LOOKING

LONELY

IN THE

FACE

Triumphant over Trials

STAR ADRIANNE WILLIAMS

Table of Contents

Loneliness is a disease cutting through the core of your spirit, to attack your soul.

I am touched by this plague called loneliness; this is the cup that I must drink from:

Hear me O Lord, Please hear my cry, and forgive me for all unrighteousness.

My strength has failed, my body is weak, every breath

I take hurts. No one cares to listen; no one cares to understand.

I have entered into my darkest hour. In Jesus 'name, amen.

PART ONE:

Who in the hell am I?

Evil Seed Planted

ﾟ♥ﾟ

O nce upon a time, there was this girl, but not just any ordinary girl, but a depressed girl, an unhappy girl, a suicidal girl who lacked hope, purpose, and ambition, a girl that everyone had overlooked and had given up on. She was left abandoned, dismayed, and rejected. Are you ready to meet that girl? The girl happens to be me, and this is my journey.

On January 19, 1974, a flickering star was born. I was raised on the hard streets of Miami, born to a paranoid schizophrenic teenage mother. She was seventeen years old to be exact. Now my dad on the other hand was a rolling stone. Coke addicted, also known as a super disc jockey at one of the most prestigious radio stations in Florida at the time. Mama was a street woman, 5'5 big afro, 135 pounds, who loved to party, drink, and mingle with different men. Due to her mental illness, she was incapable of properly taking care of me. My mother's only joy came from sitting at a bus stop for hours on end, listening to her headphones while rocking back and forth pretending like she was waiting on a bus.

Surviving her frantic episodes like roller skating on I-95 while she was pregnant with me, then leaving me in the hospital when I was born, after, trying to give me up to the neighbors shortly after my birth, it amazes me that I'm still here, so I decided to share my testimony. Everyone has a story, and I was determined to write mine down. At the tender age of four, I was considered a timid child. I can recall many nights at that young age, praying to be beautiful. According to the world's eyes, I wasn't what one would consider attractive. Dark-skinned, moon-faced with knock-knees and buckteeth (you get the picture). I was extremely shy and had a hard time socializing and speaking up. School, of course, was a struggle for me. In class, there was so much I didn't understand but I dared not raise my hand to draw any attention to myself. To make matters worse, my private school teacher was physically abusing me. Her name was Ms. J; she was this very loud, obnoxious, short stout woman with a deep, manly voice. She always wore a short gray wig and carried around this orange, thick long extension cord. If you got an answer wrong or seemed as though you weren't paying attention, she wouldn't hesitate to whack you with it. She was one of many reasons why I hated school even more; it was my enemy. My self-esteem was completely depleted therefore I toted around depression, anger, and resentment at an early age. One of my favorite stories was "The Ugly Duckling". I embraced the story in hopes that one day I would become this beautiful swan.

However, there's always someone in life who makes a world of difference, and who always has the right things to say, at the right time. This person in my life was my grandmother; we called her Grandma Dee Dee. She played the role of my grandma but in all actuality, she was my aunt. How did this happen? Well, let me break it down for you. My real grandmother and Dee Dee were sisters; my biological grandmother died while giving birth to my mom on Nov. 18, 1952, from rheumatic fever; from that point, her oldest sister Dee Dee stepped in and raised my mother.

Now Dee's mother, who was also my real grandmother's mother, was killed by a jealous lover when these sisters were around eight and nine years old. While their mother was walking from the neighborhood store one evening, the jealous lover attacked her, stabbing her more than ten times with a sharp kitchen steak knife. Still, my aunt − whom I will call my grandmother from this point on − didn't let the incident involving her mother's death overwhelm her. Filled with so much wisdom and love, nothing on earth ever robbed her of that. She certainly bared her cross, ran this race, and did not allow anything to make her bitter. She had a soft spot in her heart for my mother (her niece) and didn't hesitate to accept me as her own.

She used to lay beside me in my bed and wipe away my tears while rubbing my back. She felt my pain; she would tell me that beauty was on the inside. Back then, if I could've only flipped myself inside out, I probably would have witnessed that beauty, but at the time I had no clue as to what she meant but her words were soothing, I was just too young to understand any of it. Nevertheless, they made me feel better…About the age of six; the hip-hop era was starting to take the music scene by storm. African Americans had found an outlet from oppression and other frustrations through music and dance, which allowed us expression of pain and anger, artistically. The discovery of hip-hop helped us cope with poverty and high racial tensions.

And at that time, around the year 1980, The McDuffie riot broke out.

How could I forget it since my mother had dragged me unwillingly out of my bed in the middle of the night wearing nothing but a T-shirt, flower panties, and without shoes, we went running down the street and joined an angry crowd as they ranted with anger about killing whitey. "Now who is whitey?" I thought to myself.

An all-white jury had just released four white police officers in the death of McDuffie, a black Miami insurance agent. McDuffie was a former Marine who had been fatally beaten down while handcuffed after a police chase by a group of white police officers, who then tried to cover it up as an accident. The verdict, coming as the black community's relationship with law enforcement reached an all-time low, sent people pouring into the streets. This uproar lasted three days.

The street we lived on was prostitute and drug-infested. I would see drug deals go down and hookers selling themselves and their young daughters to clients and pimps in broad daylight. Speaking of which; I can recall this lil' girl who lived right next door to us; from my bedroom window, I could look unto her front porch, where two old rusty cars were sitting underneath a broken carport. It seemed as though the people living there were trying to convert the outside section into some sort of outdoor room.

There sat this long green leather-like couch along with a black plastic crate, which facilitated an older model television. Usually, I would look out and see different drunken men coming in and around the place. As I slept one night, I was awakened by strange sounds coming from the next-door shack, it sounded as if someone was being injured so I jumped out of my bed and ran to the window to see what was happening.

I slightly pulled back my curtain in fear of being noticed and to my surprise, there stood an old white dude with these worn-out pants dropped around his ankles having sex with the Lil girl. The small child was lying on one of the beat-up cars with her dress pulled over her waist. One of his hands that covered her mouth muffled her screams. Her mother was a few feet away sitting on the old beat-up couch; she glanced over to where her daughter was, turned her head, got up, and walked into the house.

I wasn't quite sure what was happening at the time, but I knew it was wrong, yet I regretfully never told anyone about this incident. I sometimes think about what became of the young girl. Where is she and what is she doing right now? To have had her innocence stripped away so young, I wonder if she is still alive. Could she have children? Or a family, maybe? I didn't even know her name, but I do remember her pain. Now that I am older, I completely understand what I was a witness to, and I think to myself, "What a depraved world."

While playing outside with a few friends, on several occasions I observed grown men riding by in their cars wearing neither pants nor underwear, fondling themselves. They would stare at us with this cold, deserted, perverted look in their eyes. The situation around me was gruesome.

I recall spending time at a neighborhood friend's house. She had a teenage sister called Rui. Rui's boyfriend would often come over to see her. Rui also babysat a really cute little curly-haired girl who was about 5 or 6 years old. She kept her during the daytime while her mother worked. All good, right? Well on this particular day, things took a turn for the worse. As the young girl and I were playing on the bed, Rui and her boyfriend walked in and asked us what we were doing. They then decided to lay on the bed we were playing on to watch us play. We played patty cake, rock paper scissors, and other games.

Rui's boyfriend was face up on the bed and this lil' girl, out of nowhere, climbed over to where he was and was trying to perform oral sex on him. She clenched his private part and then moved toward his penis area with her mouth. Rui pushed her head back and loudly screamed, "NOOOO!" It startled me so much that I rushed outta there so fast and never returned. I did not know what was going on, but the yell that came from Rui alarmed me so greatly that I knew it had to be something utterly devastating.

The incident was sickening, but not as personally sickening as sitting at the lunch table in my elementary school, then beginning to feel something strange going on under my skirt and hesitant to find out what it was because I feared spiders and that's exactly what it felt like, a spider or something creepy crawling in between my legs. I finally mustered up enough courage to lift the plastic tablecloth and look to see what was going on. And would you believe, there were two boys from my class underneath the table sitting on the floor, using pencils to molest me. I could not believe it. They both were fondling me with sharpened pencils. When I caught them, they laughed and ran off. It seems as if the devil was trying to plant a sexual seed in my life long before I even knew what sex was.

Another strange event took place that year. My mother gave birth to another child on June 26, 1980, my brother Christopher. I call it strange because no one even knew she was pregnant. When my grandma got word of this, she was not at all happy. My mother had already given her enough responsibility for raising me. When word came to me about the pregnancy, I didn't take it as terrible news. I was the only child, and having someone to finally interact with didn't seem like a bad idea. I thought by having a sibling around, I wouldn't be so lonely anymore.

There were a few neighborhood friends on the block that I knew, but they were a lot older, plus the activities they were engaging in made me steer left of any kind of dealings with them.

Friday nights the hood looked as if we were having a block party. Kids on the block would gather outside to sit and drink with loud boom boxes turned up blasting. They would talk 'til the wee hours of the morning. Often the older boys would get drunk and extremely horny. I was not trying to become a victim of rape, so I would get out of dodge fast when things seemed to be getting out of hand. The older females would get chased down, get caught (intentionally), and then surrender to sex. The game was; one of the boys would count to ten giving the girls a chance to run and hide. After the count, if you were found or got caught, you had to have sex with the person who found you. Although I was a little older, I was still a virgin, so I couldn't see myself involved in any game like this.

My best friend at the time, China, lived a few houses up the street from me. She was two years younger than I was, so we rarely saw each other because her parents were incredibly strict and did not allow her to come outside or do much of anything else for that matter. China had a big brother they called Bob; he had to be around nineteen years old and was browned-skinned, tall, and incredibly handsome. One day, while I was chilling around China's house, we were in her room playing with our Barbie dolls, and Bob came in wearing nothing but a towel wrapped around his waist. I can't recall exactly what he came in for, but as he turned to leave, his towel hit the floor. This was too much for my virgin eyes! I had never seen anything like that in my life (Let's leave it to your imagination as to what I saw.) but these were the kind of indecencies that I was exposed to at such an early age. I was too young and had seen way too much before I could even reach the age of ten.

My mind began to become full of questions and there was no one around to answer them. Sadness would creep up on me in the wee hours of the night, especially as I lay quietly in the dark. These moments caused my mind to become an open playground to think. "Where was my Dad?" "Why did other kids have dads and I didn't?" "How come my mom didn't love me?" "Why did she walk the streets all night?" "Maybe it was because I was ugly or something was wrong with me," I thought to myself. At that point, subconsciously I began to create a shell. Some would call it self-absorption. I called it a defense mechanism.

The year 1985 rolled around, and with the beginning of middle school in a couple of months, I felt I needed to become stronger, I was super sensitive about everything; maybe it was due to hormonal changes. I was a straight-up tomboy, who enjoyed putting firecrackers in the mouths of lizards, just to watch them blow up, from climbing tall trees to catching frogs;

I did that. Although I came off as tough on the outside, I was 100 percent cotton on the inside.

The previous year around that time, my grandmother picked me up from school and while riding home with her one afternoon, some girl was sitting at a bus stop. She watched as my grandmother's old brown Nova slowly pulled up at a red light. I glanced over at her while we waited for the light to turn green, and she stuck her tongue out at me for no reason. I had never seen this girl a day in my life, but that didn't stop me from bursting out in tears. I was sitting there crying because someone I didn't know stuck out their tongue to taunt me. I was an obvious mess.

By the time I reached middle school, my appearance had gotten worse.

My godmother, who lived right next door to us, was a church-going retired woman, who used to care for me after school while my grandmother worked, often during the week and sometimes on the weekends. She decided one afternoon to take me to the salon and have my hair processed as a surprise for my grandmother. And a surprise it was. Before the hair massacre, I maintained a good head of healthy, thick, long sandy brown hair, and a pretty decent grade at that. After the stylist was done with my head, I looked like a wet, sheep-skinned dog. Instead of the jerry curl result they were hoping to fulfill, I walked out with a very scary curl, and to make matters worse school just so happened to be the following day. Not only did I have to go to school with these crazy-looking teeth, but now I had to step up in the place as a horrendous mop. Dreadful!

While attending middle school, I didn't have many friends. While the more popular girls had boyfriends and were developed, I endured the worse end of the stick and was often teased because of the spaces between my teeth and the way I walked. My knees would knock and while standing straight, formed the letter K. I did everything I could to make myself invisible because the insults daily were unbearable. The teasing alone turned my school experience into a horror flick, not to mention I was also paper thin, had no breasts, and now had this dried-up short doo-wop-like hair on my head that fell out with the slightest touch.

My grandmother was still dressing me during this period in my life. She was extremely old-fashioned, so my sense of style was at zero percent. Talking about horrible? Butterfly collared tops, slacks with brown penny loafers, looking like Busta brown, I was busted down. As I think back, I recall the pretty girls; the ones that boys adored, they got all the attention from the guys and some teachers, too, of course. These girls wore the brand-named up-to-date clothing from Troop, MCM, and the latest Nikes, and their hair always looked as if they had just left a hair show. To top it off, they were developed and exceedingly outspoken. Mostly all were draped in gold and admired by every guy. I wanted so badly to be popular, too; I was tired of being picked on, and if I wanted a change, I knew it would take going against the grain and I wasn't ready to do that.

Finally, the school year ended, and I was still alive. Surviving the torture of seventh grade, I was given a desire to write. Writing became one of my greatest joys; it gave me an outlet for everything I was going through. I now possessed the ability to write what I was experiencing down on paper and make something of it; whether it was a play, rap, skit, or poem. Hip-hop was dominating the music scene by then, and becoming one of my greatest aspirations. I'd sit in my eighth-grade class and write an entire rap in a matter of minutes. I then became recognized for it in school, people started being nice to me because of this skill.

I didn't exactly become popular, but became pretty well-known amongst immediate peers such as my classmates. Things were looking up quite a bit in my world and I loved it. The teasing kinda subsided, too. During that year, a Puerto Rican girl by the name of Mary befriended me; she wanted me to write a rap dissing her boyfriend with whom she had recently broken up. His name was Andy. It went something like this:

Andy and his boys ain't Shiii. If there was a grave with his name I'd spit!

You get the picture. So I did that for her and thereafter our friendship grew even closer. I was so ecstatic to have someone of her caliber down with me.

Mary's looks alone could make any man's heart stop. She was light-skinned and had natural wavy, long, waist-length, jet-black hair. She had a shape an hourglass could not touch. Everywhere she went admiration would follow. I was amused by the fact that she wanted to socialize with me. As days went by, Mary and I became best friends.

Gradually changing, I started getting more into myself and finding new ways to spice up my appearance by wearing lipstick and hair extensions. Mary would let me borrow some of her clothes. Surprisingly, I was able to keep them hidden from my grandma by wearing them under my school attire (Parents beware!). My grandmother began to work a lot more due to her recent promotion. She had worked with the county for years, and it was finally starting to pay off. To my benefit, as her career demands increased, my whereabouts became impossible for her to keep up with. I took full advantage of this and started skipping school with my newfound friend Mary. Wow! Boys were looking at me now; a few of them even said I was cute. The tight jeans and short skirts became a part of my attire; I was consistently getting compliments on my legs, they were long and hairless, plus guys loved the way my lips looked. They were pouty and full. My lipstick stayed on point, and red happened to be my favorite. Finally! I lost the chubby cheeks and developed a more defined look. My high cheekbones and big innocent-looking eyes popped, tremendously standing out! Aaah, my dreams had finally come true; just like the story, "The Ugly Duckling," I was becoming a radiant swan, breathtakingly beautiful, with the power to stop traffic, you couldn't tell me nothin'. Mary and I were unstoppable; we were the original dynamic duo, strawberry, and chocolate to be exact! Hello!

It was just another day when we decided to skip school as usual and go to a store called Zayers. Zayers at that time was something like what Wal-Mart is now, a one-stop shop. We walked up in there and were getting a lot of suspicious looks mainly because we looked so young, I'm sure those folks knew that we were supposed to be in school. Our grown get-ups meant nothing; people saw right through us. Mary and I proceeded to the back. As we passed the doll section, I spotted the Cabbage Patch dolls, a super hot item at the time. I may have been acting grown, but I was still a kid at heart, anticipating womanhood but at the same time still enjoying playing with dolls.

I don't know what had gotten into me that day, but I decided to steal one of the dolls, even though I had about ten different kinds already at home. As we were leaving the store, I walked with the Cabbage patch doll stuffed under my shirt, and then I spotted a large bright yellow tote bag hanging on a clearance rack on the way out. I felt it would be less obvious if I stuffed the doll in the bag before exiting the store. Did I mention that the bag was bright yellow? I took a cut, put the doll inside, and carried it like a tote. When we reached the exit door, there stood a large security guard already posted there as if he was waiting on us. He forced us back inside, I'd never been so embarrassed.

Security took us into a small room and searched us, and to my surprise, Mary was doing a little illegal shopping of her own. Her pockets were stuffed with make-up and other small cosmetic goodies, but I'm sure I was the dead giveaway and got us both caught. This was not good at all; we had to be released into the custody of our parents since we were underage. OUR PARENTS!!! My heart fell to the floor as the store's security called my grandmother's job.

When I arrived home, after she was finished with me, I couldn't sit for a week. That was the worst whopping of my life. She explained in derogatory terms that she wanted me to end the friendship I had with Mary. It was the first time I had ever heard my grandmamma curse.

After that incident, the friendship between Mary and I automatically started deteriorating. I was told that she got into serious trouble and suffered great consequences. Her father was extremely strict and did not play at all.

On Jan. 19, 1988, my fourteenth birthday arrived. My family was not into throwing big parties, just a nice dinner, a couple of friends, and some cake was the tradition. My grandmother's best friend, Ms. Ann Hidges, a well-dressed successful director for the Department of Human Services whom I considered my aunt, brought me a pair of tight denim capris as a gift. Now this was a woman with style and grace. She was tall, well, and undeniably stunning. She kept the money and drove a gold four-door Audi. I was ecstatic that she was the one to hand me the gift because I knew I wouldn't have to hide wearing them. And let me tell you, I got her money's worth out of them jokers. I wore them to the store, I wore them to the park, I wore them to school, and probably wore them to bed a time or two, no seriously. Every female has a special pair of favorite jeans that she loves, the ones that compliment her physique and hug her every curve. Ladies, you know what I'm talking about. But I think I took my love for them a bit too far; I overdid it maybe just a little too much. I wore the seam out of those bad boys. Wore the blue off of 'em. The inside of the thigh area had turned from blue to white in a matter of months. I'd wear them and when I arrived home later that day, hand wash them; and let them air dry, so they could be ready for the very next day. I know this sounds sad, and it was. Still, you couldn't tell me nothing when I had this pair on, don't judge me; I was too proud.

Wild Child

⁓⁓⁓⁓⁓⁓⁓

One scorching hot Saturday afternoon, I was so bored. I was growing immensely of weary playing with dolls and watching the Disney channel, so I decided that I'd go outside and supervise my little brother, run around the yard, and fool around. I grabbed a seat on the hood of my grandmama's old car, a light blue Regal. Dolls weren't the main attraction anymore. I was looking past plastic heads and fake bodies that couldn't move. I still wanted to play but was inquisitive about another kind of game, which involved a real body; I had discovered a new interest. This guy they called Red seldom came on our block to holla at some of the older boys who lived in a huge house down the street from us.

They were all brothers who lived in that house. Let's see… There was Hoog, the sly, cool, cute one that almost every girl wanted. Beeda, the troublemaker, Hoog's big brother, and Ro, the oldest, who I always thought was gay, because he had a really funny twist to his walk as if his legs were gonna break off, he was soft-spoken, on top of that he had a curly perm. Hoog, on the other hand, was the youngest. I used to have a strong crush on him, but when I found out he had a thang for my friend Mary, I pushed the pause button. Beeda was the middle child, and in one word, a "terrorist," who was the ringleader to the weekend -night block sexcapades I previously mentioned.

While sitting in my grandmothers' car that day, Red and Beeda were walking by my house, I'm assuming they were headed to the neighborhood store not too far up the road. Red was around eighteen years old. Fine! Light-skinned! Stood about 5'11, had a nice smile, and athletic body.

He also had these mesmerizing light brown eyes. As he passed, my eyes met him, and a warm tingling feeling came over me. I had never felt that before. Someone once said that the tingling feeling is "our common sense leaving our bodies" Although he did not say a word, I remained captivated by his presence and stared in their direction until they disappeared. Why didn't he say anything? I guess he felt I was too young; nevertheless, I could not get him out of my mind. I anticipated his return from wherever they had gone. What would I say when he walked back by, I wondered. I was so nervous. How would he react if I said hi? I was thinking of running into the house, taking off the clothes I had on, and putting on those birthday Capri's; yes the Capri's! But I wouldn't have enough time, and I didn't wanna miss him. I could see them approaching from a distance; my heart raced; my stomach bubbled. I then positioned myself, and waited until he got closer and said, "Hi Red." "Was 'sup," he responded. My heart dropped to my feet, employing a slight case of the bubble guts. I couldn't believe I was that bold, I spoke to him. As he was walking over to me, I overheard Beeda say to him, "Man, that ain't ripe yet." I was so glad that Red ignored him. We finally exchanged numbers. At that moment, I felt like a kid in the candy store; you know the feeling when you get someone's number you always liked and in your head, you keep replaying how the whole episode happened.

After multiple conversations on the phone, Red was aware I was a virgin; he seemed so understanding. He told me in due time, he'd teach me everything I needed to know. I agreed and told him I would be leaving for Orlando in a couple of days and that I'd be gone for a week. My grandmother had planned a family vacation. She was taking us to Walt Disney World for the summer; I was looking forward to this trip because we had been talking about it since the previous year. I was so surprised that we were still going because my report card had F3F all down the row.

A day before we were about to leave, my brother decided he wanted to play with matches. My grandmother was in the kitchen, and I was in the den located in the back of the house, plus Tony, my Grand mama's son, was there. He was out in the yard chillin'. Now I had a slight appreciation for Tony. When I was maybe three or four years old, he walked in on my mom about to bust me across my head with a broomstick and was able to grab the stick before she could hit me with it. The stick was only inches away from my head. Tony and I were pretty close back then; however, our bond fell short when I started feeling myself, meaning becoming less controllable; and getting older. But, I still had a lot of love for him.

Well, all of a sudden I started smelling smoke but didn't think too much of it, cause my grandmamma was in the kitchen. I figured she must have burned something. Seconds later, her son Tony ran inside yelling, "THE SIDE OF THE HOUSE IS ON FIRE...! FIRE!" I said, "What? Fire"?! I rushed to where my grandmother was. Tony continued shouting "GET OUT THE HOUSE!" All I could think was "Where's my brother?" Crazy thoughts raced through my mind. I was frantic. I then ran into the side of the house, where I saw the smoke coming from. The fire in that room was blazing. By then Tony had everyone out of the house, I was chronically coughing, and I felt someone grab my arm; I could not breathe and thought I was going to die. I didn't know who grabbed me, but I whispered "Where's Chris?" Once safe outside, I saw that Chris had already made it out as well.

That was a sad day; we lost virtually everything in that fire. While looking through the rubbish, I was able to salvage a few dolls I owned while others were burned to a crisp. I cannot put into words how upset I was. However, I didn't care too much about the house because it was infested with plenty of roaches and rats, but I still had a love for my dolls; they'd been with me for years. Looking back now, I realize how selfish I was, too young-minded to comprehend that our lives were spared that day. I truly believe; you have to learn, how to be grateful.

Thank God my godmother who lived next door opened up her house to us while the insurance company assessed the damages. While there, I snuck on the phone to call Red. He hadn't heard from me in about a week, and I'm sure he probably thought that I was still at Disney. When he answered, he was elated to hear from me; we planned to meet later on because my grandmother was going out of town that evening on a business trip and I knew my godmother would let me do as I pleased.

"You want some grits, suga?" she asked. My answer was always NO because she would make grits for breakfast, lunch, and dinner; one thing I did not wanna see while I was there was another grit. She finally went into the room to take her evening nap; being sneaky, I picked up the phone and called Red back. I told him to come over and to meet me outside.

Once he arrived, we hit up a shed located in the backyard, which belonged to my godmother. It was set up like a storage unit where she kept her washer and dryer. I took a seat on the dryer, while Red stood in front of me with his hands on my thighs. He asked a thousand questions in regard to what went down on the day of the fire. I told him that my lil brother found a box of matches, hid under the bed, and started striking them, and next thing you know, the entire house was engulfed in flames. He seemed concerned, attentively interested in what I had to say; to show his affection, he gave me a long embrace, held me tight, and assured me, everything would be ok. This was the first time I'd ever been held by any man; it felt really good, too. For the first time in my life, I felt secure, accepted, and needed. Red gently kissed me on my lips, looked me in my eyes then asked me if was I ready to become a woman. Like an innocent child, I gave no verbal reply but shook my head.

I witnessed his whole demeanor starting to change. His aggression frightened me. First, he lifted me off the dryer and laid me on the hard ground next to it, next he savagely ripped off my jeans and panties. I struggled and struggled with him a bit but was no match for his strength. Finally, he pried my legs.

I looked at him with a morsel of fear as he unbuttoned and pulled down his pants. There was no turning back; I could feel my heart vigorously pumping in my chest. I was petrified!

Nervous! Confused! Before I could even get a word out, he was inside of me. I felt a sharp discomfort in my stomach, it hurt, and he was not taking his time, viciously biting and sexing me. My back was pressing against the hard cold concrete! That part alone was killing me! The pain was excruciating! I must have called his name over 50 times but got no response. He turned as cold as ice; ignoring my cries, as I yelled, "Stop!" I begged and pleaded with him; he seemed to be zoned out and was not hearing me. After it was all over, he glanced at me then got up and left. I just sat there torn, shocked, throbbing in a pool of blood, crying my eyes out. It felt like I was living a nightmare. I didn't understand why I was bleeding from my vagina. No one ever explained this part of sex to me.

With no one to turn to, there I was, helpless, alone, struggling to get up, pressing my way into the house to bathe. While in the shower, I wept like a baby as the blood trickled down my legs. I tried to collect my thoughts as to why. I could not believe he would use so much force knowing I was a virgin. When I got out of the shower, I needed someone to talk to.

I hadn't seen or heard anything from Mary, so I called her and told her what had happened. Of course, she was more experienced than I was. And when I told her what had just taken place she sounded elated. She stated that since I was a virgin, my cherry popped and that the blood was a normal thing. Cherry, What Cherries? I was oblivious to what she meant. The only cherries I had any knowledge of were the ones my grandmother brought back from the grocery store. She ooed and awed, but to me, it was no laughing matter; I was suffering and had just been deserted by my first love.

Fathers, the ones who are not an active part of their child's life, must not know the damage they are doing to their children by not being there, especially to girls. They have no clue about the emptiness their daughters feel, the confusion, the yearning and wanting you, carrying around the nagging desire to be accepted, by someone, anyone. She'll do anything for a man's affection. The first one that comes along that tells her she's pretty or makes her feel loved; she falls for him without a parachute. She'll start accepting relationships regardless of how destructive they are due to her lack of self-esteem. She loses her self-worth in trying to find that love she never had, only to try and fill that void within her, and she knows something is missing. What's missing? Daddy! Mother can only do so much. Soon she will be asking, "Where's Daddy?"

Grandmas can only do so much, aunts can only do but so much. I needed you, Daddy, and you were nowhere to be found. After that episode, I desired to pick up the pieces of my life and keep it moving. Would you believe that after that situation went down, Red had the balls to try and converse with me?

Entering ninth grade, I attended a school called Miami Northwestern, which happened to be a few blocks away from Red's house. On several occasions, he would catch me walking to school and threaten me if I didn't skip and go with him to his house. When we got there, all he wanted was sex all day until school ended. I'd get dressed; grab my book bag, and then walk back home, most times in pain. He seemed to have complete control of my mind, and like a dang fool, being young and naïve, I'd go with him; mostly every day. He told me how much he loved me, how he would never leave me. And last but not least he told me something that I had never heard before; he said "That I was beautiful." Whatever he was selling, I was surely buying.

See, fathers, if you do not get in your daughter's mind, then someone else will.

Red used me sexually and abused me emotionally and physically. If he felt I was out of line or I rejected his proposal to skip school he'd hit, bite, or choke me. I was under the impression that he was my boyfriend and this was just how men behaved. There was no knight in shining armor coming to rescue me from his clutch, no father nor father figure for that matter nowhere in sight. No daddy-daughter dances, no butterfly kisses. Who was there to show or teach me how a young lady was supposed to be treated? There was nothing. Nothing but pure torture and a lot of sex from a person who I thought loved me. I caught whatever he threw at me. This gentle flower was growing wild.

Being that I was still so young, I felt intimidated by the older females living on my block. They were well-developed, some having cars, and they seemed to have it all together. There I was still trying to grow breasts. Soon word had gotten back to me that Red had a thing for one of those older chicks that lived around the corner.

I also heard that he was saying negative things about me behind my back. I was told he would say things like "I didn't satisfy him and how he wanted someone else," and that he was ready to be with a real woman. I was deeply hurt when I heard this; on top of that, my self-esteem was already at an all-time low. When I confronted him about the rumors, he slapped me so hard that I was surprised that I still had eyes in my head. I wanted to be done with him, but my mind wasn't right, plus I was an emotional wreck. I didn't feel strong enough to leave him, and if I did, I felt that no one else would ever love me, remember this was my first love; the love of my life.

I had this nagging insecurity in which I assumed that if my dad left then surely every other man would, too. Serious trust issues can set the mind to sabotaging any good thing that ever comes your way.

Well, the dreaded day for me soon arrived! Red had recently gotten a car. He came over to my house to pick up me and my friend they called Ducy, also known as tartar teeth. He had one of his buddies in the car with him. We all decided to go to the park to hang out. I can't recall exactly how I met Ducy, but we were cool. Ducy was this jet-black female with a killer body. I can recall times when I used to stare at her face super hard and try to understand what guys saw in her because she kept so many.

I couldn't grasp the fact that they were diggin' her cause she looked like a troll and wore a pound of baby powder on her neck.

I told her a lot about Red, I confided in her so it didn't seem too weird for her to act so anxious to meet him. She was exultant as she climbed in the backseat of his old black Riviera. I looked back at her, and she had this sinister-looking smile on her face. I didn't think too much of it at the time, but I did notice Red constantly looking in his rearview mirror as we drove.

Arriving at the park, she decided that she was hot and took off the short-sleeved jacket that accompanied this skin-tight black jumper she had on. Her big breasts were all over the place, and Red, being disrespectful as he was, couldn't keep the little remarks and gestures to himself. Of course, I was too afraid of him to confront him with anything, so I stayed silent.

Ducy was a loudmouth, and she was also extremely confrontational. She happened to spot one of her old flings and started stirring up junk with him. I walked in the other direction. I was not about to fight anybody's battles especially when they had initiated them. So I grabbed Red's hand as I walked away while she continued to carry on with this dude about God knows what.

When grabbing Red, he seemed a bit hesitant to move. "No, he didn't!" I thought to myself. I could not believe it. He defended her by running up to the dude like he wanted to fight him. Didn't he bring a friend for her? Why can't he handle this then? Red didn't even know her.

Red's homeboy was still posted up in the car smoking, obviously unconcerned.

Eventually, the dude she was fighting with backed down and went his own way. And I watched as the love of my life tended to my friend, at the same time I was being completely ignored by him. He left me standing there, humiliated, and again deserted. I was so shocked I couldn't say a word. He'd broken my heart once, and a broken heart can be mended, but this time I was crushed, and when something is crushed, it can't be repaired.

That was the state I was in that day. My world was spinning 300 miles per hour, and I walked back over to the car only to be ridiculed by his homeboy. The night was approaching, and I was ready to go. I looked in the distance for Red but didn't see him or Ducy. At last, thirty minutes later, they came walking to the car, I asked no questions and even offered her the front seat.

The ride home was an incredibly quiet one. That was the last time I had heard anything from Red, until one day while watching the evening news, I noticed his car surrounded by a swarm of police and helicopters. From what I understood, he had led them on a high-speed chase. I could not believe what I was seeing; the police officers had their guns drawn as he was lying on the ground in an act of surrender. I can't remember all the details but he was wanted for strong armed robbery. I gave up all hope of us ever being together again after this incident. I never knew love; would hurt this bad; the worst pain I ever had.

Sour Sixteen

By the time I was sixteen, I had put a capital R in the word rebellion. I was completely out of control, not listening to anything or anyone anymore. My grandmother couldn't handle me, and no one else could either, for that matter. I was convinced that I was grown. Entering my tenth-grade year, my black book looked like the Yellow Pages. I became heartless. I found out that I had this special power that lay between my legs that was beyond good, and as long as I didn't give it up so easily I could dictate any situation with any man. I was a user and a manipulator. I cheated on every guy I was with, in and out of relationships, and was carefree.

Yet, I remained mentally bound by depression. The night was the worst because all my emotional scars would resurface. I felt trapped within my own body and hated the dark; everything was so silent at night. I could hear myself think, further, I could not stand that. My past troubled me, and issues in my life disturbed me. I wanted to run away again, but not to just end up in my backyard again like before. I wanted to get far away from myself, I didn't like myself, besides, I hated the person I was becoming, but I didn't know how to escape it all.

I will never forget the day I finally mustered up enough courage to call my dad. He was at work at the time. He worked for one of Miami's hottest radio stations. The station was promoting the Salt and Pepper concert and was giving away free tickets to the ninth or tenth caller. I just wanted to talk to him to see if a relationship between us could be established; in addition, I wanted those tickets, so I called him. Over the phone, his tone seemed a bit nonchalant, and kinda egotistical, but I overlooked that. I went on and told him who I was, and he did not seem too impressed. He sounded like he had just heard from me minutes ago. Now, this was a man I hadn't heard from in over ten years.

The last time I saw him I was around five or six years old. My mother took me with her to his job so she could fuss and fight with him over some money. That day she got her teeth knocked out of her mouth. Yep, my dad hit her so hard, that he knocked her teeth out. That was the last time I'd seen him. The convo over the phone wasn't what I had expected, so I ended up asking for the second thing, I was calling for which were the concert tickets. I was so surprised and excited when he agreed to give them to me because he had never lifted a finger on my behalf in all of my sixteen years here on earth. Of course, he wasn't going to bring them to me; I had to find a way to him, but I did. While on the way, there were butterflies in my stomach, I couldn't wait to hug him and perhaps start mending our relationship.

Despite the slightly cold phone call, I still had hope. I set aside all the anger I felt toward him for not being there. My time had come; a moment that I felt would change my life for the better, getting to know my father. We finally arrived at the radio station. I jumped out of my friend guy's car with great anticipation. I slowly walked to the radio station's door at the same time fixing my hair and clothing. I was nervous but eager to make a great impression. I stood at the door for a second, sighed, and then knocked; this was so surreal, yet it all felt so right! As I waited, short visions of our reunion filled my mind. I wondered if I looked like him. Was he short or tall? I could hear music playing from the inside. Before I could knock again I heard someone on the other side ask, "May I help you?" I asked if Jimmy G was there. "One second," he said. Next, the door cracked open, an arm reached out with two tickets in hand, and then immediately the door quickly slammed shut! Bamm! And that was it. Wow! He didn't care to see my face; he didn't want to hug me, not even a "Hello." Nothing! My soul was sad, and my heart bled. My dream was over. Rejected, abandoned, cast out, that pretty much sums up the way I felt that day.

During the rest of my teenage life, after dropping out of school, my family and I moved to another area. Red was finally out of my life for good because the judge sentenced him to 10 years in state prison. At that point, I wanted nothing to do with a man but started having strong urges for a child, a product of me that would love me unconditionally and someone I could give that same love in return, never really giving much thought as to how I would support it or myself. But I was determined. It happened on July 13, 1991. I gave birth to a beautiful little girl. She had the most gorgeous eyes that I'd ever seen.

Her father was another story, I met him while at a bus stop over the summer, and we instantly became really good friends. He grew up on the rough streets of Spanish Harlem, N.Y., and was nicknamed Rico. You guessed it. Puerto Rican, 5'11 nice hair, gorgeous light complexion, and medium built, but there was one problem, he was WITHOUT SWAG, and I mean he had no swag at all! He was also kinda corny and a bit goofy, too, but he looked tantalizingly good.

Come on ladies, you know when a man is fine; we overlook all his little mishaps. We feel like we can fix 'em up. Not long after we met, I wearily tried to change him into the person I wanted him to be, constantly telling him to wear his pants like this or buy a shirt like that.

My grandmother, lo and behold, agreed to let him move in with us so that he could be a present help with his child. She was not at all pleased with the pregnancy and on numerous occasions had tried to talk me into getting an abortion. My grandma ended up buying a bigger house for a good deal located in an area called Brown-Sub. Rico and I ended up staying in a fairly large room that was an addition to the house. He claimed that he always wanted to be a family because he knew what it was like growing up without one. He was an orphan whose mother and father had been brutally murdered when he was younger. He told stories of abuse, and how he had to sleep on top of old apartment buildings while living in N.Y, as a child. I think our similarities of not having a mother or father drew us together. We both came from broken homes, which allowed us to relate to each other's thoughts and overall hardship. We thought that we could somehow fix one another.

When things were good they were great, and when they were bad, it was like hell. At times we got along, but most times we fought like pit bulls and stray cats. It was no longer working out between us. When our daughter was about eight months old, I grew weary of the whole family thing; I thought a child would bring love and happiness like an Al Green song. Instead, it brought screaming, lack of time with self, and exhaustion. I was tired, I didn't love Rico anymore, and I wanted out. I didn't sign up for this. But did I? I loved my child, but this was a bit too much. I was getting older. I started to reflect on my whole life. "What was life"? Was this all it was? I felt as though living was over before it ever began. To soothe my wounds, and escape from Alcatraz, I fell into the arms of a green-eyed bandit, named Benny. He stimulated my mind richly.

Benny was my liberation, someone who I felt that I could share all my dreams with. Of course, he was notably handsome; dark-skinned with piercing green eyes because I wouldn't have it any other way, but despite that, he was a great listener, something Rico wasn't. Benny and I remained friends, and I would occasionally sneak away to indulge in conversation with him, desperately needing a few laughs. I felt bad because I knew that Rico was head over heels in love with me, but at the same time, I didn't feel all that bad because I knew that he was also conversing with someone else behind my back. His beeper went off one morning while he was in the shower. I called the number back and some girl answered the phone. I quickly hung it up; there was no caller ID back then, so she couldn't call back. I never questioned Rico about it because I also was sweeping my dirt under the rug. So, I felt my actions were justified. But what's in the dark always will come to the light, and the spotlight will soon shine on me. After another night out with Benny, I came home about the same time as I usually do and Rico was home early from work. He had this insane look in his eyes. My heart almost popped out of my chest, the truth being guilty people are always on the edge. Before I could get a word out, he started yelling and screaming about me cheating. His face turned blood red, and then rage suddenly took over. This was my first time seeing him like this; all I could say was "Huh? What, another dude? What dude?" I thought to myself, "How in the world did he find this out?" Someone had to have tipped him off, and I had a clue as to who it was – my so-called friend, regrettably one of my new best friends.

See, I've had my share of friends, and by being in denial, took me a while to understand that most women can't be trusted. And you can't tell your friend everything especially things about your love life. I learned that the hard way.

Anyway, I finally calmed Rico down by telling him the truth about Benny, that he was a friend and nothing more, well maybe not the whole truth. After that, I got my so-called best friend on the phone, and in a split second, my mouthpiece became a sawed-off shotgun. I fired and reloaded and fired some more. I poured my entire wrath out on her in that one phone call, unleashing rounds of affliction that I had built up over the years for females who I knew, did whatever they could to take away what was mine. A drug called the white horse took my daddy; an addiction took my mama, which was alcohol and the streets. A trick took my first love, and a liar named satan was trying to destroy my life.

Later that night, I settled in, kissed Rico, and again told him how sorry I was. I was under the impression that our fight was over, afterwards, I laid down in hopes of a peaceful night's sleep; it had been a long exhausting day.

During the night, I would sometimes roll over on my side and rest my leg across Rico's waist while we slept. On this particular night when I tried to do it; he wasn't there. I immediately woke up; looked around and didn't see him anywhere in the room, so I got up to see where he might have gone, and what I saw sent me into total shock. It was pure unadulterated terror! Rico was on the front porch lying in a pool of blood.

I rushed into my grandmama's room and told her to call 911. She got up to see what was going on and became hysterical! She grabbed my baby who was asleep in her crib and went back into her room to call 911. I stepped out on the front porch and went over to console him until the ambulance arrived. I looked around to decipher what may have happened. He could barely talk and was going in and out of consciousness.

I kept telling him, "It's ok baby, you'll be all right." My goal was to keep him alive; I did not want him to fall asleep.

I soon realized this man had cut his wrists. Blood was profusely gushing out both of them. I looked to my right and a couple feet away saw the instrument that he used to create this heinous scene. A sharp pocketknife emerged in blood. My goodness, why was rescue taking so long to get here, I whispered. As we frantically waited for them to arrive, he was losing enormous amounts of blood and kept going in and out of consciousness. The more I tried to comfort them, he repeatedly said, "She cheated…She cheated on me" up until the ambulance arrived.

I could not believe it. I couldn't believe the havoc a so-called friend had placed on my family, but was she really to blame? Or was this all my fault? This was certainly a life-changing experience, and I told myself that I would never cheat on anyone ever again. That did not last; I guess it is true about what they say "Once a playa; always a playa."

Rico eventually got better as time went on. My grandmother then told him that he needed to move out. I was sorta relieved; well, more bittersweet than anything. I knew that it was pretty much the end of us. I also knew that I could not be with a man who would take his own life. It was just the fear of coming home and finding a person dead in the living room whether it was my fault or not. I couldn't live with that. I was putting my life in perspective and didn't want any more interference, and he was a big one. To top it off, I grew weary of playing house.

PART TWO:

The Path to Death

Another Chapter

By the time my daughter was two, I felt the urge to go back to school. My grandmother, now retired due to an illness, supported my decision. She was a firm believer in education and didn't take it lightly. She grew up in a time when doors were completely shut for African Americans and she grieved to see blacks throwing away so much opportunity. She also played a major part in the civil rights movement in which she volunteered her time to see a better tomorrow, for those reasons, going back to school became one of my greatest desires. The only issue was I knew I could not stay in Miami. I needed to get away, far away, where no one knew me, disconnected from all the problems and troubles that continuously haunted my present environment.

When starting fresh, it's wise that we don't lug around old luggage.

I decided that I would sign up for Job Corps, and ended up choosing the Morganfield Kentucky Campus. I had this vision that it would be an all-white school, a super country, and everyone would mind their own business. I expected no drama and freedom from attractive men, or at least would be free from the ones I would be interested in. My grandmother agreed to watch my daughter for as long as I embraced this journey for a better future. I soon was accepted at the school and once I arrived.... Behold!!! There was not a white in sight, students flocked from all over the world and they were all black...not one white person. Not A ONE. I was SHOCKED! "Am I in Morganfield, Kentucky?" I thought.

The school required that all students, once they were assigned to their dorms; take a physical and HIV test. That thought chilled me to the bone. I had never had an HIV test done, and I was not even trying to go that route. One thing in life I knew I did not wanna hear was... "I'm so sorry Ms. Williams but you are HIV positive." The notion alone almost stopped my breathing.

I told the administration that I was refusing the test, but they informed me that to remain in school it was mandatory. My nights were horrible, the trepidation of going to the campus infirmary to take a test. This was probably when I found God. Isn't it funny when we find ourselves in need of a miracle or a way out of a dire situation, we tend to become super-spiritual? I remember praying, "Lord please, I don't want HIV, please help me Lord, and I promise I will never have sex again; Lord, I'll go to church every Sunday. I'll do whatever you want me to do, Lord, just please! NO HIV. Please!"

I was begging for my life. Contemplation of unprotected sex over the years took hold of me. After crying and praying, the very next day I built up enough courage and got tested. The waiting period to retrieve my test results was a Monsta. I was so nervous; that I couldn't think or focus on my schoolwork. Every time my classroom door would open, I thought that it was someone sent by the infirmary to get me out of class so they could notify me of my results. Whew! Talking about paranoia? That I was, I tried to shake the feeling and couldn't. It was horrible.

Weeks passed, and I didn't hear anything back from the infirmary. I was starting to feel good about it all, until the day while walking into my room the dorm captain stopped me, as I was entering. She told me that the infirmary contacted her and told her that I needed to go over there. My heart dropped to my feet! Go over there? NO THANK YOU! I dodged that bullet for a while until the dorm captain stepped up to me again and explained that the school would deduct from my allotment if I didn't comply with the rules.

See, Job Corps did not only teach but paid you to get an education, literally! It wasn't much, but it was more than what I had.

I can still recall that slow dreaded walk to the campus clinic to retrieve my test results. My stomach was constantly bubbling, my eyes were a bit wider that day, and my nerves were shot to hell. I walked into the clinic, signed in, and for some reason, it felt like everyone there was staring at me. I sat in a corner and waited for them to call my name. While I sat there, I assumed my nerves got the best of me because minutes later I started contemplating ways of escape. As soon as I stood up to execute my exit strategy, the nurse called my name and asked me to follow her. I entered the room, and she told me to "have a seat." She told me that the doctor would be right with me. As I waited on the doc, I picked my fingers uncontrollably. Then he walked in… "Hello, Ms. Williams," he exclaimed with hesitation. "Hello Doctor," I replied. My mind went blank. He spoke nothing of an HIV test, only of an important appointment I'd missed for a scheduled pap smear. I was puzzled yet ecstatic. "Aren't you going to read my test results?" I asked. He answered "Oh," and then he smiled as if I had surprised him. He reached for my records which were annoyingly sitting on the desk in front of him, and before I got the chance to brace myself, he said that my HIV results were negative. Whew…huh…What!! Negative! OK, play with it! Praise God! I was so relieved, I felt like a brand new woman with a new lease on life, overjoyed, that I WAS HIV-FREE!

Funny how when things seem to be going right how easy we are to forget all those promises we made to God when we thought we were in trouble. Here's the problem…He never forgets, and you'll soon end up in another hole.

In Job Corps, I got a lot of attention from the guys. Every other day there seemed to be a few guys wanting to get more acquainted, but I wasn't interested. None turned my head because they came off as a bit slow to me. I was this city slicker, sharp, seasoned with a lot of game. And these dudes were so lame. I felt like I could run circles around them, that was until I noticed a man they called E. This E was popular; he was unlike any man I had ever met. He was so real; he had other dudes at Job Corps wanting to be him. They would imitate his walk, style, and dress code. He had a mouthful of gold teeth; twelve to be exact, and contrary to the pullouts that boys walk around with today, his gold's were permanent. Back then, if you were caught with pullouts in your mouth, you would become the laughingstock of the entire school. Times have drastically changed. E was indeed swagalicious, muscular build, 5'11, and unlike anything I had ever seen. Job Corp guys turned into wild beasts over girls coming from Miami. Miami girls were irresistible and somewhat different to them. Of course, I was no exception, but it was E who caught my attention, and eventually, I caught his. I was cute, desirable with an impeccable "A game" to say the least. One thing I'd learned mostly about some men is; that they admired innocence; they seemed to thrive off knowing that a female needed them. I also learned early that too much nagging turned them off as well, but a woman who holds her own and still fits him in as a necessity is a major turn-on. So the game was on, and I needed to play my position, if I were to win E's heart.

Keeping in mind that I'm the female, he's the male, and he yearns to feel like the man that he is at all times.

Pretty boys in my book were not at all appealing to me, plus I'd already had my share of that dealing with my baby daddy. I liked my men, rough, careless, and borderline disrespectful. Any man that stepped on me had to be a real man, a man's man. And E, in my eyes, was the true definition of it. We started kicking it hard on campus. If you saw him, you saw me. There was so much jealousy in the air. Many females desired to be "the one" but didn't cut, yet he did have an ex who tried to make my life miserable by spreading rumors and occasionally running up on us with drama, but I didn't feed into it. She was hurt because he'd left her for me, and I knew this, so I applied a little mercy.

After a while, random people would come to tell me things about him, but I did not wanna hear them. I knew that he was probably messing around with other chicks but I did not give one ounce of care. Nothing mattered because at that time

I felt I had the prize and everyone else around me was just jealous of us. I fell in love with his sex, which was on point, and we had lots of it.

A year later, I graduated from Job Corps feeling a sense of accomplishment. This school was what I needed. It instilled in me that I could do anything if I just put my mind to it. As for E, he had already finished and had left six months prior. As he happened to be from Miami, we vowed before he left to stay in touch. When I reached home, we immediately hooked up, and as years went by, we grew closer. We ended up being together for eleven years and within this time; he became my second baby daddy.

Although while in Job Corps I prayed and prayed to God for him to be the one, this was surely not a match made in Heaven. To tell you the truth, my time with him was the worst and most painful 11 years of my life. Cheater, liar, manipulator, you name it. This ugly pattern in my life went from rotten apples to sour oranges. We women become dangerously defensive when blinded by love. We take people's warnings as jealously and swear everyone wants what we have. We refuse to see that what we got ain't even all that good.

E and I, despite all the chaos, ended up getting our place, staying together only for the sake of being comfortable; all I can say is "bad move." Most times, we couldn't even scrape together 50 cents to buy a soda.

Employment was scarce for a convicted felon. Oh, did I mention he had a record? In the past, way before I knew him, he and his boys decided that they were going to shoot at the police. He ended up serving three years in prison it, and businesses were not taking any chances. After giving up hope on him finding a job, I ended up auditioning for a local popular strip club in Miami called the Rolex. I nailed it, but when it came time for me to put down on stage in the presence of hungry men, I ran out the back door; still in costume looking like a chicken wearing white lace and high heels. I don't judge or would never knock a person for doing what they gotta do to survive, but the only way I could've got through that performance was if someone else would have let me borrow their whole body, face, and brain. This was not my forte.

As the relationship dragged on, I realized I wasn't content. I was so tired of him staying out late, not coming home 'til the wee hours of the morning, and blaming it on work. He would flirt with my friends right in front of my face. And, ladies, you know that's one of the most embarrassing feelings in the world, cuz when we are around the girls, we try to act like we got it going on. We make it seem like we got our man wrapped around our fingers. We pretend like we got it all together when we don't. We hate being the laughingstock of the party, the dumb buzzard amid the vultures.

Some nights while he showered, I admit I would go through his cell phone and write down as many unrecognized numbers I could get, then call them the next day. Lo, and behold! You guessed it…They were all women. I'm assuming one of them must have had really small cute feet because I remember getting into an argument with him one morning, and all he did was bash my feet, talking about "how big they were" and so on. This was new! He'd never done that before. Come on now! My feet? Really? We were about in our ninth year together and out of all the arguments we had he never mentioned my feet. Where in the world did that come from? BINGO! He was comparing my feet to one of his jump-offs.

The Breaking Point

When a woman has low self-esteem, she is already at a breaking point; anything could make her crack, and I finally did. No one said it better than R-Kelly: "When a woman's fed up, it ain't nothin' you can do about it".

Our last two years together were as cold as Alaska, the darkness intensified. Often a dead silence hung between us. Ignoring each other was just a small indication that our relationship was over, I was suffocating with three kids. The first baby daddy was a deadbeat, and this one was a nightmare. I felt so empty inside, just plain sad, but I wore a fake smile every day to throw everyone off. I hated living together, and everything about him sickened me. His voice rang in my ears like, loud screaming annoying sirens going off without warning. His natural scent disgusted me to the point I felt like regurgitating. The void in my life was chronic, drained to the max with nothing left to give, and worn-out. I felt I loved my children; but did I really? There was no love left in me, not even for myself. Was it possible to love anyone else without loving yourself first? I had given up. Numbness was an understatement, as the sign of lifelessness emanated from my eyes. Here I was, once again in a hopeless situation.

Yes, you can live with a man and still experience loneliness, you can also be married and have friends around you constantly and still be lonely. Loneliness feeds on depression. Depression keeps loneliness alive.

I can recall many times I hung out with friends, laughing, eating, and pretending to have a good ol' time while internally dying. I had no one to talk to. I felt no one loved me. Self-pity sunk in, and I was in the bottomless pit. I walked around with the notion that if my mama and daddy didn't love me, then no one ever would. This was the reason I gave up on relationships. I disengaged from the world. I created this humongous wall and isolated myself, letting no one in. That is where I took refuge; the wall I had built became my security. I felt safe, guarded, and protected at last.

I took no crap from anyone, and my tolerance level was sub-zero. You never know what a person is going through until they explode. They all of a sudden just snap.

Thinking back on all the unfulfilled promises I had made to God, I knew I would find myself in another ditch. Better yet, a deep hole this time around. This grave was too cavernous to climb out of on my own. There was no light here; all I could do was feel pain.

It pierced my very soul. I'd lie on the bed every night and replay my entire life over and over again. What had I done to deserve this deck of cards? I wanted it all to end so I prayed to God for Him to just take my life. I always knew if I committed suicide, I would go straight to hell so that selfish act was out of the question. I grew up in the church; I knew the rules, but I didn't know Christ. I asked the one who gave me life to take it away. E just made matters worse, but I must admit he provided for his children. I had no money, the rent was behind, and I'd lost so much weight I couldn't fit any of my clothes and certainly couldn't afford new ones. I looked like a hot mess. The saddest part of all was I didn't even care.

During the last year of our relationship, we kinda knew that it was over although we didn't speak much of it. The connection between us had lost all reception. We tried one last time to rekindle what we lost by having sex. It was gross. I was in tears, my body was numb while he was on top of me and he didn't even know it. My self-worth no longer existed.

In the back of my mind, I knew he had found someone else. His recent cell phone bill arrived in the mail. I looked over it and spotted an out-of-town number that he had been calling numerous times a day. Their talk time was off the charts. One hour here, three hours there, both within 24 hours, so I figured it was something serious. Days and days went by. I quietly sat in my room, zoning in and out in deep thought. The walls appeared to be closing in on me. I slightly lifted my head and glanced over into my vanity mirror. And at that moment I realized that I Was LOOKING LONELY IN THE FACE literally.

Then the phone rang. It was my grandmother. I didn't want to speak to anyone, too ashamed and too disgraced. Everything she'd once told me was coming to pass. I could not stand to hear the words "I told you so" from anyone right now. She warned me time and time again about this one, and the obvious was I didn't listen.

In the spring of 2004, a movie called The Passion of the Christ hit theaters. I had no one to go to the movies with, of course, so I figured I'd go alone. This movie had major production behind it plus the previews were epic. I mustered up some strength, found something to wear, and went on my way.

I watched the movie and sobbed the entire time. Jesus Christ, the Son of the living God died and shed his blood for me? For me, this was pretty mind-boggling, but I knew it was real. Suddenly, the answer struck me like lightning. Everything I'd heard preachers speak of before started to make sense. Mentally, things were put in perspective as though my understanding was suddenly awakened.

For God so loved the world, that he gave his only begotten Son, that whosoever believes in him, shall not perish. But have everlasting life.

John 3:16

Wow! My drive home was life-changing, I cried out, beating the steering wheel, apologizing to God for everything I had ever done. I completely surrendered that night. That was the moment I realized I could not do it by myself I just could not anymore. I wasn't strong enough to face this life on my own. Therefore, I finally surrendered. I would think about the movie, cry, then cry some more. I had hit rock bottom and there was nowhere to look but up. If there was a better life waiting for me, I wanted a piece of it badly.

Not only was I ready to live, but I was also ready to live for the one who had died so that I could live. JESUS

Finally, I arrived home and located a Bible that had not been touched in years sitting in my room closet. My kids were away on break at their grandma's house so I decided to take this time out to read it. This was the first time in a long time I was happy to be alone. I opened the book, and the words seemed as if they had come to life, literally. It was as if they were directed at me. It seemed so personal. The verse I read was…

Though my father and mother forsake me, The Lord will receive me

(Psalm 27:10)

A Father to the Fatherless a Defender (Psalm 68:5)

Those words brought so much comfort in my time of grief.

E arrived home that night and saw me sitting at the dining room table in tears. These were tears of joy. I contemplated how I was going to tell him that he needed to move out, knowing we both had pitched in money for our home, but I wasn't happy anymore and I had to let him know. He needed to know that I could no longer be a part of his plan. Fornicating and lying in bed with a man who was not my husband was now a thing of the past. But how could I tell him? I feared the outcome. And this is what the devil wants so that you'll never be able to move forward, trying his best to stagnate the plans that God has for your life by keeping you stuck, in bondage. Worry, another trap of the enemy, consumed my mind, things like; who would take the garbage out? Who's gonna help take care of my kids or the bills? Anxiety rushed in like a flood. I had made him my god; he had put up a certain security for me for so long until I didn't know how to break free. I was enslaved, trapped by convenience, like so many women who stay with a man not necessarily because they love them, but because the arrangement is comfortable. Nevertheless, I knew that I had to make a decision.

If I was gonna live for God, the renewal process wouldn't be easy, but it was vital if I was gonna attain any kind of future, so I built up the nerve to tell him what was on my mind. I told E to come over and sit down. I explained to him that I had given my life to Christ, and I wanted out. He seemed puzzled as if he didn't understand what I was saying. He gave me this side eye Stevie J looks like "OK" (If you don't know who Stevie J is, just Google him.). However, just as I expected, he barked like a dog, insulted and threatened me. His argument led me to believe that he was under the impression that I couldn't make it without him, and there were doubts in the back of my mind that caused me to believe this for a moment also.

For the message of the cross is foolishness to those who are perishing, But to us who are being saved, it is the power of God. (1 Corinthians 1:18)

I couldn't blame him; he just didn't understand. He eventually moved out and ended up living with the female, he had been calling daily. It was cool because I was getting on with my life as well. Coming out of that funk, living seemed different. I was breathing, and the sun appeared to be shining again. My devotion was not only real but obvious. Although no one told me that things would get a little shaky before they got better, the adversity that comes with following Christ caught me completely off guard; I was so unaware of, the testing, the trials, and troubles that take hold of new believers were no joke. I was an immature Christian enduring some serious storms. During the whole process of transitioning from death to life, I was determined to hold on. Satan threw any and everything at me. He used people and my finances to try to sink my ship, but I stayed afloat under some severe attacks. I knew God was testing and refining me, and it hurt, but it hurt so good. This was a different kind of pain.

But who knows the way that I take; when He has tested me, I will come forth

as Gold. (Job 23:10)

I awakened one morning and cleaned the house, getting rid of all my old clothes and shoes, selling outdated children's books, pawning TVs, computers, and any other electronics I could find around the house, as I desperately needed the money. Pictures that brought no Glory to God went out as well, including beautiful paintings of Chinese prostitutes (geisha) and a shrine that held a statue of Buddha. What in the world was I thinking? Back then I was compelled by Asian art, but all of it had to go; if the Lord was against it, then I was, too. Please understand that anything you put before God becomes your master. When we bring certain artifacts into our home from out of the world, some of these things can attract demons, and you can involuntarily invite spirits into your home by having certain kinds of images on clothing, pictures, watching and listening to secular music, etc. If it looks or sounds like death, then that's what it probably represents.

Of what value is an idol, since a man has carved it? Or an image that teaches

lies? (Habakkuk 3:18)

The money made from the pawnshop was all of $250 petty bucks. There were two outfits left dangling in my closet, which was all I owned. I lost it all without care. The repo man crept up like a thief in the night and dragged my 2003 dark blue Honda Accord off into the night. Two weeks after that, my lights got cut off; three days later, the water followed. I asked E's mom to keep the kids because my living conditions were not looking good. Thinking things could not get any worse. I arrived home one evening to find an eviction notice on my door. The more I tried to keep my situation concealed, the more I was exposed. I wondered how long the notice had been there and had any of the neighbors had seen it; such humiliation. Folks, who knew me, the ones waiting on my downfall, had a field day, especially since I had to wear the same attire repetitiously. I wasn't mentally prepared to become the talk at my enemies' dinner tables. I was embarrassed and regretfully unable to provide my kids with the necessities in this phase of their lives. I chose to remain hopeful never firing back at anyone who mocked me, on the other hand, I was praying for my enemies and that was no easy task. Not only was that the most difficult thing I had ever done. But I knew then, a change had to come.

Then my enemies will see that the LORD is on my side. They will be ashamed that they taunted me, saying, "So where is the LORD—that God of yours?" With my own eyes, I will see their downfall; they will be trampled like mud in the streets. (Micah 7:10)

All these words I was reading didn't seem at the time to be helping me out much either; I thought I was doing everything right, and I'd even stopped cussing. What was going on? "Does God not see that I'm in need?" I wondered. I read that He was present in a time of trouble, that He was a God who knew what I needed before I even asked. Well, I was in big trouble and did everything I knew to do. I had all this power and did not know how to activate it. The Holy Spirit said to me, "Keep praying and don't grow weary in well doing. In due season, I will reap my reward," and so I did.

Months went by, and then suddenly, out of nowhere, my whole situation turned around. The doors shut tight just a few years ago and started opening. Favor poured on me like rain. You never know when God is going to act, you just need to be in a position to receive, keep faith, and know that He will.

From Dust to Diva

Hallelujah! I thought I heard the angels singing. I landed a job with one of the biggest car rental agencies in the country. During my waiting season, I was also planting seeds; I just didn't sit around but got out and sowed, filling out applications and when reaping season came around I got the call. It's ok to have faith and believe God for something but Faith without works is dead.

As the body without the spirit is dead, so faith without deeds is dead.

(James 2:26)

The restoration was in motion. After losing a plethora of rags, gaining the hottest fashion was only the beginning. The big old floor model TV that was sold with all that other junk simply made room for my new 56-inch flat Samsung HDTV. The repo man did carry away my Honda, which gave way for the platinum-colored Nissan Altima; it wasn't a Benz but it was clean, loaded, just three years old, and under 40,000 miles – on top of that, I was able to pay cash for it, which meant payment-free. Slowly drove off the lot, all smiles, bumping "Picture Me Rolling" by Tupac. Wide-screened TVs, Dell computers, clothing, and food were the least of my worries. Child, please!

As for my kids, I could not do enough. I went all out! If it was in season, they had it.

That same year I was able to move my mother to a more upscale neighborhood and drop brand new furniture for her all in the same day. Deep down, I knew that was something she always wanted and I could not see anyone else making that happen for her.

Things were undeniably looking up. It didn't matter where I went; all eyes would be on me; and getting compliments left and right was a part of my everyday routine. I loved the admiration, it was nice for a female to see me coming, and watch her as she clenched her man a little tighter due to her insecurities. "I DON'T WANT YOUR MAN SWEETIE; I DIDN'T EVEN WANT MY OWN". I became cocky, and the distractions caused me to lose focus. I was a Christian but was becoming worldly, outright fixated on the external and losing complete sight of the Eternal.

Although I could afford pleasurable things, stuff only gave me a temporary fix. Gucci and Loui became great friends of mine, but they didn't satisfy me for very long. For example, I would go to the mall and get all hyped up over a pair of designer frames, purchase them, and forget I even bought them a month later. The more stuff I had, the more miserable I became.

I found myself longing for more of God. I know without a shadow of a doubt I'd fallen in love with Him. He lavished me with all these great gifts to show his faithfulness. He not only gives you everything you need, he also gives you a lot of your wants – double for your trouble in other words. As I sat and glanced in the rear view of my life, I could not say anything but "WOW! God is good!" all the time.

Jesus said "In this life you will have trouble" and let me tell you, He never lied. It was preparation time for winter because my season was about to shift.

In July 2008, my beloved grandmother's illness took over and she passed away. Doctors said she had a hole in her lung due to excessive smoking over the years despite her quitting before my last child was born seven years prior. That was too late, for the damage was already done. The spiritual strength she possessed allowed her to hang on longer than usual, but the physical side of things couldn't hold up anymore. To this day, I wish she would've stopped smoking sooner. I was so distraught over this tragedy. Many folks tried to console me, but nothing helped. I was so tired of hearing the most popular line ever written when someone dies "She's in a better place."

I understood all of that to the fullest, but it quenched my selfish desire, as self-absorption fueled my anguish. I needed her with me, despite knowing her suffering in her last days concerning her lungs, and what she would encounter on an everyday basis just to breathe, I still wanted her here in the worst way. She was essentially the only family I had left. No hurt, no despair, no sting in life, compared to the loss of my beloved grandmother. She will forever be missed. RIP Hagins, you are eternally loved.

If you assume satan cares that you've lost a loved one or that your life is turned upside down at any point, then you are blind. His ultimate goal is to destroy you. He will hit you even harder in your weakest moments. This enemy will not ever let up, although he may flee from you for a while; as soon as he senses vulnerability in any form on your part, he will rush in for the kill. We are in a constant spiritual battle, and often we don't even know it. It's all the more reason we must remain equipped with the full armor of God. Yes, the Lord fights our battles, but if we didn't have to fight sometimes and stand firm amid a war, why would we need His armor?

Be strong in the Lord and in His mighty power. Put on the full Armor of God so that you can take your stand against the devil's schemes. For our struggle is not against flesh and blood, but against the rulers, against the authorities, against the powers of this dark world, and the spiritual forces of evil in the heavenly realms. Therefore, put on the full Armor of God, so that when the day of evil comes, you may be able to stand your ground, and after you have done everything, stand. Stand firm then, with the belt of truth buckled round your waist, with the breastplate of righteousness in place, and with your feet fitted with the readiness that comes from the gospel of peace. In addition to all this, take up the shield of faith, with which you can extinguish all the flaming arrows of the evil one. Take the helmet of salvation and the sword of the Spirit, which is the word of God. (Ephesians 6:10-17)

Self-pity resurfaced. I sought to be comforted, as feelings of worthlessness shook my foundation. The Holy Spirit was there all along, but me refusing to be comforted, gave me the ability to ignore and disregard him. This means to quiet the spirit by indulging in sin, to pay no attention to his convictions. Sensual thoughts and sexual urges rushed in with full force. Wars in the heavenly realm broke out; spirit and flesh were raging, powerfully battling against each other but the flesh was winning this time around. Why? Because I was giving into temptation, I declined to put on the full armor and only wore parts of it. Instead of running to the Word for strength, instead of leaping into the arms of the Lord prayerfully, I wanted to run into the arms of a man, but not just any man but one who I knew would satisfy and fulfill this mega-sexual appetite, every inch of my lustful pleasure, all of my shameless cravings without restraint.

I now realize that the Lord calls for faithful intimacy, the same urge you have when you long to be with someone (in the flesh) is similar to the longing we should have for Him (in the Spirit).

The particular individual I had in mind was a vet, sexually charged and without limit. When I made the call, he seemed to have arrived in just seconds; my knight in dark blue Levi's and a pair of size 11 retro Jordan's rode in prepared and ready for the takedown. He must have been speeding on that horse. Anyway, my thoughts were now a reality, and there was no turning back now. This sexy 6-foot-2 chocolate brother greeted me with a long embrace; I could feel that he was happy to see me. We hadn't seen each other in a minute but communicated here and there online. I had such a huge crush on him in high school but was too shy to speak up then. We bumped heads again later in life and exchanged numbers, but nothing serious came about. He instantly became a friend with benefits. As he stood in front of me, I proceeded to undress him with my eyes, he smelled so good. All the while, red flags, bells, and whistles were going off, but I decided to ignore all caution. I lived in a townhome, so we headed over to the staircase that led to my bedroom. Attempting to walk up, we didn't make it; right then and there on about the fourth step, things got really hot and unquestionably heavy. Before I could take another step, he'd stopped me in my tracks and got on top of me. I made sure to wear a dress for easy access. Wasting no time, he unbuttoned his pants and slid off my panties. He was so passionate and attentive; his Ralph Lauren cologne filled my nostrils, which made trying to hold back even harder, I just couldn't resist him any longer. As he delicately kissed my neck and gently bit my ear, my body waved like the ocean; I was soaked. Every stroke was long, hard, and deep. I screamed aloud and as a result, I birthed full-blown sin. Afterward, I felt horrible, like death in a bottle, guilty, and dirty; I was disgusted with myself and completely disappointed.

When he left, I felt separated from God, and outright overwhelmed with shame. I heard satan laughing in my ear; he scoffed at me and reminded me that I was of no value.

Crazy how he convinces people to do things and after it's done he condemns. He'll take you on this major high; suspend you in mid-air, just to drop you off a 100-foot cliff. The higher you go with him, the longer and harder the fall. He tempts us all in different ways by remembering our weaknesses and then using them against us. He'll never tempt me with crack cocaine because I don't have a drug problem. The temptation is always congruent with our flaws and weaknesses.

I could not believe I went there, though. I knew better, plus I had been doing so well. Guilt is the result of sin after you have tasted the Lord's goodness. The intense yearning you have to fulfill the flesh is the same level of intensity that God wants us to yearn for Him, on a spiritual level.

Therefore we must long to be with Him, crave to draw nearer by developing a more profound relationship with the

Lord, and thirst to be in His presence instead of man's. Not long after this sinful encounter, I repented, but take note: the Lord does chasten those He loves, but He only does it to correct you.

I had lain around for days feeling like a desert on the inside, and my poor soul ached badly. I so needed His restoration, to be watered, to bask in His peace. I wanted to be filled again.

The only way I knew to acquire this was to get into the word; nevertheless, to fall deeper in love with Jesus. The more I read, the more I drew from the living water. Power and healing replaced sorrow and shame. Once we ask for forgiveness, we are forgiven immediately, but we must learn to let go of the guilt and forgive ourselves, if not, we will carry around this heavyweight, a weight that will soon affect our physical health and stunt our spiritual growth, giving the devil a foothold in your life. God is not holding your past sins against you and you shouldn't either. LET IT GO!

I, even I, am he who blots out your transgressions, for my own sake, and remembers your sins no more. (Isaiah 43:25)

When things are off track in life, we often do one or two things. We find ourselves isolated or clinging, we'd rather cut off from the church, family, and caring friends, or cling onto something that can become destructive in the end, relatively food or alcohol, maybe a man or woman, another kind of drug, sex or even friends, none of which are capable of making you whole. After that last rendezvous, I did a lot of soul-searching and what I found was astonishing. I learned I didn't truly love myself. Yes, I was in a better financial position, able to treat myself to the temporary luxuries of this world, but to tell you the truth, most times I was hiding behind insecurities, pain, disappointments, loneliness, and emptiness. Material wealth frequently gives us the liberty of saying "Look at Me" without having to verbally express it. It gives us this small validation of accomplishment.

God wants you to get to a place where you know that you are blessed; with or without specific substances, and understand that anything good that manifests itself in the natural is only the result of the blessing. During my inner search and asking God to help me learn how to love myself, I noticed that my impatience made waiting on Him difficult to appreciate the rewards He had already given me for trusting in Him. By focusing too much on the next stage of my journey and anticipating what God would do next in my life, I was missing out, neglecting what He'd already done, I lost track and was incapable of savoring any milestone or special moments. Anxiety robs us of our peace. We must learn to be content and embrace where God has us at this second, or we'll soon become ungrateful and unappreciative, overlooking the smaller things with anxiousness about getting to the greater.

Starting over with a clean slate, I cut off many folk who called themselves my friends but had ulterior motives. Looking back, I remember the lowest point in my existence. No one was there; I couldn't call a soul and get a measly $50 when I was down. My cell phone was not ringing on the regular, nor was anyone waiting in line to rush to my aid. There stood only me and the Lord. I am positive that when trials and tribulations arise, God shows you who's going to have your back. You may have people in your life who are takers; all they know to do is take. Be careful, this is another avenue to emptiness as well. If you find yourself always on the giving end, eventually it will drain you, not just emotionally, but spiritually and physically, leaving you capsized with zero left to give. Your Spirit needs to be renewed and refreshed daily. It's possible to start off having a good week and by Wednesday you don't know whether you should go right or left. It's just that serious; we need our daily bread. If you ate food or drank only once a week, you couldn't make it, and your physical body would most likely collapse, so imagine being fed once a week spiritually, your inner man would be starving.

But whoever drinks the water I give him will never thirst. Indeed, the water I give him will become in him a spring of water welling up to eternal life.

(John 4:14)

Many nights while facing my loneliness, the pain was so great that I felt like I was going to die, but instead of making calls, surfing the web, or reaching out for instant self-gratification, this time I called on God. Making sure He had not forgotten me, I asked Him in my conversations with Him to remember me. I wondered did He still had someone in store, handpicked by Him just for me.

Years ago, when I'd first given my life to Christ, God gave me a vision.

This vision was of a man he had chosen for me to marry; also in this vision, He showed me my past and how His hand delivered me from all of Satan's devices and demonic traps set up to destroy me. Then I saw the present, of how He carried and lifted my burdens without me knowing that He was even there. Lastly, a glimpse of the future, my future, and it looked amazing. I was astonished. I was looking at the man He decided to give me before the creation of the world. He was beautiful, alluring, and well put together, I was partnered with someone who loved me, and not only that, this was no ordinary man; he loved the Lord, was handsome, and was significantly wealthy. God loved me so much that He has chosen to give me one of His best.

I am bone of his bone. Flesh of his flesh. With all modesty, when I glimpsed him, I instantly knew his name; known by a few for his artistry and has a decent following. Digesting this in the flesh, I would say that this man is too good to be true. Not only is he attractive, but he's also incredibly talented. I remain genuinely humbled by the vision. I'm not sure if I was even praying for a husband at the time, but God in all His grace and mercy saw fit to let me see what was ahead. The vision is so large it seems unattainable, but I know without a doubt it was from God. So I wondered if had I gone too far by dipping in sin. Had I killed the promise by giving myself away to another, knowing all of what I knew?

We often think that God has given a promise then later revokes it when we don't walk on a fine line.

Well, that is so far from the truth. The truth is when we are faithless, He is still faithful, as long as we REPENT, get back in his will, and continue our walk in obedience.

God knows us better than we know ourselves, and although He wants the very best for us, He's not surprised when we mess up. Before He told me anything about my future, He knew my beginning and my end. If you are a believer or planning to become one, practice waiting on God, the Lord's plan in His timing.

Some of us women, not all, often end up settling due to the flesh constantly urging us to give up on waiting.

If you think it's impossible to be unequally yoked with a Christian partner, then you are wrong. The Creator is the only one who knows which Christian will be suitable for you, which one will complement you, and which one will take you to greater heights in ministry for His glory.

If you are working on marriage, then you are indeed working on a ministry as well. Marriage is ministry; it exemplifies the relationship Christ has with the Church. In the process of getting to know myself better, I stopped depending on superficial ideas and notions this world supplied, falling into the systematic traps of thinking like "If only I had this or more of that I would be happier." Self-examinations lead me to ask some deeper questions. I dug deep, asking things only the Holy Spirit could answer like "Why was I so unhappy in the first place if the Joy of the Lord is my strength?" Furthermore, why was I looking to share my life with another person when I could not even get along with myself? I learned that happiness is a choice that depends on occurring circumstances.

Joy on the other hand relied on everything unseen, an array of unfailing eternal hope that pointed towards Christ and his death on the cross. So by focusing on trying to pacify the outer and disregarding the inner, I would only bring misery to any person that entered into my life at the present. This also being one of the reasons why so many marriages fail, people are linking up with grown kids.

These are women and men alike, with opened wounds who haven't allowed the healing power of God to close up their painful past, sores, bruises, hurts, and so on, and the result?

Their partner ends up with a broken-wounded mess, instead of a whole person. Y'all may not like me, but that is the truth.

How can we expect someone else to ease our pain if his or her pain remains relevant? Another person will not make you complete. The happiest couples consist of two intact people.

Another one of satan's strategies is to make you think that the world is against you. If he can cause you to believe that something is wrong with you, then he can bring to the fore feelings of desolation, later turning it into depression. Depression happens to be a serious illness. It is the root of despair, the epitome of loneliness.

Loneliness is a type of bondage that may cause you to act out of character. Frustration, impatience, isolation, and guilt are some of the feelings experienced as a result of loneliness. There were days I wanted to sleep time away so I wouldn't have to face life's realities. If I slept, then I didn't have to confront anything. Trying to sleep away your problems is moreover a sign of melancholy. It cripples you. No one is strong enough to overcome loneliness on their own, and most people never will admit they are in this situation to begin with. They'd rather cloud the truth with an illusion. People are great at playing pretend, behaving like they're ok, wearing a mask and please believe; most of them are the life of the party. Have you ever noticed that when people hear about a person they knew committed suicide, their family and friends, even the ones closest to them would say that "They were happy or they had a bright future" or something to that effect? It's because this is the impression they had given to others. Therefore, no one ever saw it coming.

This plague does not discriminate. It does not matter if you are a college student or a wealthy businesswoman/man; it is a universal issue that affects millions worldwide.

Whatever has triggered the problem, whether it was something from your past, childhood, a disappointment, divorce, or some sort of setback, you must acknowledge it and face it dead on, as cancer is detected in its early stages, giving no room for growth or spreading.

I'm from the gutter and was raised by a typical black family that taught whatever happens in the house stays in the house. The brainwashing that started in my earlier years canceled all chances for me to reach out to anyone. Then later, due to embarrassment and having a false sense of pride, I suppressed those painful realities by throwing on daily masks and parading around like, all was well when it wasn't. It is time to stop all the nonsense, and look loneliness in the face!

Are you ready to get naked before God?

Raped, neglected, never feeling good enough, rejection, betrayal, abandonment, insecurities, and abuse were stems that led to my loneliness. I laid all these ailments before His altar.

Cast your cares on the Lord and he will sustain you; he will never let the righteous fall. (Psalms 56:13)

Are you ashamed of your actions or an unwise judgment call you made that ended up being one of the worst decisions ever? If it has you in an unhealthy isolated state, then you are headed for disaster.

One of the greatest gifts God has given us is each other. This may be a good time to pray and ask Him to lead you to a Spirit-filled church or become a volunteer to help the sick or homeless. Focusing on others and their needs can help with the healing process because then you don't have the time to pity yourself. There was an era when I felt like true friends didn't exist anymore. This world has grown increasingly evil, and you may think everyone is out for themselves, but you would be surprised at how God can turn things around in your life.

He's able to send someone genuine who will not judge you, someone who can be an enormous help. Among all the seeds of evil in this world, the Lord does have a remnant in the earth, so don't fall into a mindset thinking that you don't need anyone. It is a lie from the pit of hell! Every last human being needs someone. If this were not so, there would be no need for people to even exist. We are the helping hands of God.

Someone recently asked me, "Why is there so much corruption in the world, so much killing, babies starving to death?" On that occasion, I could not answer that question, but now I can. This planet lacks love; the ice cubes of hate have crept into many hearts and have left them frozen. Humans have become numb to receiving love, so we definitely cannot give it; that which makes us incapable of loving ourselves as well. Not only in America but in many countries all over the world, people have closed their ears to what God has to say. Jesus taught love. Two of the greatest commandments in His word are: "Love the Lord your God with all your heart, mind, and strength" and the second is "Love your neighbor as yourself." I can now tell that person – the one who sarcastically asked me about the condition of this world and where was God – that the earth is sick and the only way it will ever heal is if we turn to Him inclusively, The Lord simply says:

If my people, who are called by my name, will humble themselves and pray

and seek my face, and turn from their wicked ways, then will I hear from

Heaven and will forgive their sin and will heal their land.

(2 Chronicles 7:14)

As you can see, God has laid out his remedy before us; but who is listening?

Now, turning 40, I can honestly say that I am content with my current condition. Even though I am a single mother, I'm also a dedicated writer who's focused on getting me together for my future mate. We as women regularly scream out, "There are no good men left" and about how we want "a real man." But are you being real? We should be focusing on bettering ourselves.

What if the man of your dreams were to suddenly enter your life? Could you truthfully say you are ready to be the woman that he may need in his life? Ask yourself. Is my credit straight? Am I set to share my space? Do I have a bank account? What can I bring to the table? How would I make him a better man or be a help to his life? Do I love myself? I'm not even speaking on a sexual level because a man can get that anywhere. And the most relevant question of them all is "Are you ready to submit?"

These are just a few questions to ask yourself. This alone will give you a better outlook as to what you are looking for.

This way we won't fall into any of Satan's traps when he tries to tempt us with things that will ultimately hurt us. Trusting in God is not solely about believing, it is also a waiting process.

Desperation may cause you to hook yourself up but don't blame God when the relationship comes crumbling down. It's easy to fault someone else for our mistakes after the damage is done. The signs are always there, but we choose to ignore them because we want what we want when we want it. In every relationship I've ever been involved in, I recall the Lord throwing up the warning signs before it got any deeper.

Sex with someone only will last a little while because before you know it, emotions start kicking in, so booty calls don't necessarily cut it, especially with females. We can try to have the mentality of a man and attempt to do what he does, but we cannot control the feelings we have for someone. Girl, please…we are not built that way. Sex, for us, complicates things. You can try to think like a man all you want, but the fact is that until you grow a penis, YOU WILL NEVER BE A MAN! A woman can't do what a man does and still be considered a lady.

When sin enters your life, despite the fact you have been forgiven by God, dealing with the consequences still has a major effect. Don't believe me, read the story of David. David was a man after God's heart. He was chosen; a king to be exact. He started walking with Lord then somehow fell short. David lusted after another man's wife, and to make matters worse got her husband killed. To sum it up, David ended up repenting, but he still had to pay the cost for his actions.

There are many people out there who are living with diseases, unwanted children, divorce, painful regrets, and even death, mostly all because of the result of sin. God has forgiven and forgotten our iniquities, yet the reality of sin's cost is still highly relevant.

Lately, I have been focused on Jesus; it's those moments when we take our eyes off him that put us in grave situations.

My most recent admire was a rehabilitated thug. He stepped up to me as I was exiting my vehicle. He had major charm and confidence, but because I'm better equipped to wait on my mate, now I do not waste time anymore unless God has something specifically he wants to say to an individual through me, and in this case, He did, so I ended up giving this man my number.

Immediately I heard the Holy Spirit say, "This is only for a season." This young man needed a little encouragement at the time. He was rather down on his luck, and the Lord used me to speak life into his current situation. After a couple of conversations over the phone, he started getting hooked on the anointing, which resulted in him expressing how he felt about me.

I said to myself, "Oh Lord."

I tirelessly reminded him that I was not looking for anything serious. He explained that I was a very rare woman, one whom he could see himself with in the future. His kind words were very generous. I am humbled enough to appreciate nice gestures from anyone, but I had to conduct an audit of his life. This may sound harsh, but this guy was asking me out on dates and didn't have a vehicle. I don't entirely have a problem with public transportation, but two grown adults over the age of thirty trying to make it to the movies and/or to dinner on the bus is not a good look. By the way, yes, in fact, I own my vehicle, yet I feel like it is the man's role to come and escort the woman out on a date. Excuse me for being too old-fashioned.

Another thing that made me pump my brakes was his current dwelling condition. He'd previously told me that he lived with his aunt, so that meant to spend time together I'd have to be more accommodating due to his current disadvantages. He was not the one for me.

My standards may be high, but not uncommon. Is having a car and maybe a place of your own too much to ask for starters?

A person coming into your life should not be a burden but a help. I'm not saying that we shouldn't help folk; Like I mentioned before, I do believe we are put here to uplift one another, but when you're always on the giving end of any relationship or friendship, it can become a bit draining. Plus, why should I lower my standards when God Himself has raised them? Loving yourself is so prevalent. And when we don't consider ourselves worthy we're willing to accept foolishness and go for anything. Accepting whatever, does not, and will not cut it with me anymore.

So until the chosen one comes, I will continue to live a life pleasing to God and not settle whatsoever. On days when loneliness is heavily weighing on my heart, I try to stay off the Internet. If you are connected with online sites, blogs, or social networks, you might run across images of friends' or acquaintances' wedding videos or pics, which may make you feel like you are in a world all alone. You subconsciously start comparing your life to theirs, especially if you feel you're in some way better or think you're more deserving than them. That's Pride, watch out for this! Jealousy and envy may be at your front door. These two words are similar but show up differently when in action.

Envy is a feeling of discontent or covetousness about another's advantages, success, a possession – in other words, someone who wants what you have and/or tries hard to be like you.

Jealously, on the other hand, is an anger you have against a person who seems to be enjoying life. If you've ever experienced someone hating you for absolutely nothing or vice versa, this is a hater attitude. Both undeniably can lead to a mental uneasiness that follows resentment.

Loving how God made you is an essential part of loving yourself.

Embrace things about yourself rather than complain, from your big feet, and curly or kinky hair texture, to your skin complexion. You are you and there is no one else in this entire world like you. If you don't love yourself, then why are you expecting someone else to love you? Take positive notice that you are uniquely different from anyone else in the universe. Keep in mind you were not a mistake.

For you created my inmost being; you knit me together in my mother's womb. I praise you because I am fearfully and wonderfully made. (Psalms 139:13)

Try joining a gym; we get so busy in our lives that we neglect the things that matter the most…ourselves. Don't allow petty things like not having the appropriate workout clothes, or wondering what others may think, to steer you from making better decisions for yourself. If you're anything like me, I didn't wanna look like a movie star every time I went into a gym to exercise. I did not need the added pressure of worrying about what man was looking at my butt when I passed by and what he thought about it thereafter, but I let nothing stop me and found a local all-women's gym in my area.

That's right, all-women, so days I'm not in the mood to spruce up like a superstar, I have the freedom of going in looking like a ragdoll if I want to. Being in that kind of spot alone took a burden off.

It's easy to get caught up in your feelings and have them sway you in many directions; it's never wise to act on our emotions. Think about it; if we get too caught up in the way we feel, nothing will get done half of the time. And by that being said, there are no excuses in life; the ones that we create are the only ones that exist.

The Bible states "We should love our neighbor as we love ourselves." Question: How can we possibly be capable of loving anyone else if we don't love ourselves first? If you've let yourself go, don't hesitate to find that local gym in your area and start putting forth effort by getting in shape getting back in shape, or just simply getting healthier.

Working out is a confidence booster. If you discover it's too hard to get motivated for your well-being, how do you plan to stay fit for your mate when he or she comes along?

Healthy lifestyle changes start with you. Decisions you make in life should benefit you first, then others will be able to benefit from you and your experiences.

Look in the mirror and speak positively to yourself daily. Continue to convince the mind even if the eyes can't see it yet. Most real godly men I've spoken with are in search of godly women, yes! however, some are not willing to settle with a woman who only has the spiritual side of her life together.

The real ones, who are worth it, want the full package with everything in order, including mind, body, and soul.

What some of these men have expressed to me is that they meet women all the time and the body is right but their spirit is in shambles or the soul is right but the body is broken down. They said, "Most love God and their worship is beautiful, but after one conversation, they realized that they're still broken and need God's help to heal."

Like with any wedding, a bride takes months or sometimes years to prepare herself for that special day. She desires everything to look stunning and perfect, from the theme, the colors, whether it will be held in or outdoors, who the bridesmaids will be, the invitations, and of course, the dress. She's enamored during this time and somewhat anxious. Still, she refuses to give up on the necessary arrangements that need to be made. You probably will never see a bride showing up on her wedding day, dirty, visually abused, hair undone, bursting through the chapel doors cussin' and fussin'. Well then, the time and patience women put in preparing to become a bride is the same way God preps us. He wants to make us beautiful, a bride without spots or wrinkles, lacking nothing, and not just with outer adornments but more importantly with the inner fixings.

PART THREE:

The End of Me

Silent Tears

On some mornings when I would awake, I felt as though someone poured out a bucket of emptiness into my soul overnight while I slept.

I so wanted to roll over and cuddle in the arms of the person I loved.

I craved the voice of a man saying, "Good morning baby" deeply whispered, motivating me to get up and cook an all-inclusive breakfast and have it fed to him as he lays there in bed.

However, my harsh reality of being alone was way too real on this day. I turned on my side and stared at my colorless white wall intensely grabbing my partially flat oversize pillow and holding it as if it were a human.

Instead of offering up my usual morning praise to God, I just cried and cried.

The only thing my spirit yelled out in that second was "When God? When will this bout of loneliness end?" Internally, I pleaded for Jesus' help. I was having one of my days, and it was not pretty. Shortly thereafter, I calmed down only to experience immense comfort. God in His mercy released yet another vision to me, one in which I saw myself as a child on the beach, walking along the seashore with Jesus. Strangely, I couldn't see His face being that both of our backs were turned. I recognized it was Him by the white fluorescent robe He wore and his dark brown, shoulder-length hair, the same way a parent holds on to a child's hand, in this same manner, the Lord was holding on to mine as we walked along, seeming to be no older than five years old in this vision. There was such a sense of peace in our fellowship. It became apparent that things around me easily distracted me because every time I saw certain seashells wash on the shore, as well as other people on the beach doing their own thing; I would snatch my hand out of His to run over to pick up the shells, forgetting He was there. Jesus would patiently wait until I was done with whatever it was I was doing.

Each time, I'd return to Him then place my hand back in His and we'd continue walking. This routine became repetitious. Whether it was a seagull, a sailboat, or the ocean's waves, repeatedly I stopped walking with Him and marveled for a few moments at any distraction. Jesus is so patient, He never complained; every single time He would wait for me, always accepting my hand.

After the vision was over, I wept, I knew what the Lord had shown me, it was the reality of His children's condition, the present state of their existence.

This world is an enormous place; with countless options to choose from. It is full of distractions at every turn. Before you have time to take another breath or look up, there's another new thing introduced to the world, some other invention or gadget that people create, to try to take your mind further and further away from God. But Jesus, being the kind, meek, loving Savior that He is, long suffers for us, kindheartedly accepting us back each time.

He is more than fascinating. The lust of the eyes and the pride of life grab our attention momentarily but the span does not last.

Love is the only thing in this world that is everlasting.

I will tell you, that this journey of mine hasn't been easy but it has been well worth it.

Learning how to love and forgive others, including yourself, is an ongoing process. A daily dying to one's thoughts, reasoning, and emotion is no walk in the park.

To ride this thing we call life can only be accomplished with help from someone who is greater than you, stronger than you, and most importantly wiser than you. This person happens to be the Holy Spirit, the Spirit of God who leads us into all truth. Nothing nor anyone else is capable of enabling us for this stride in living holy.

These are just a few truths I sought out during my soul search. If it had not been for the Lord on my side, where would I be? I can answer that; I would be lost, powerless! Even worse, destroyed!

You mustn't believe the lie of the devil when he says, "You are alone in your pain and suffering" convincing you that no one cares, as he pushes you towards suicidal thoughts and defeat. He thrives off this hopeless state of mind.

Believe you are valuable, that God has a major plan for you, and that you are not forgotten. There is a world full of souls out here that need you. If people in your surroundings don't appreciate you, then move on.

Seek out folk who will honor you.

Guard your heart against nasty evildoers. Encountering malicious, self-centered, disloyal distant people is bound to happen, so watch out. Insist on letting no one change your character. The word of God even speaks of this:

Because of the increase of wickedness, the love of most will grow cold, but he who stands firm to the end will be saved. (Matthew 23:38)

There is no wonder why we must be like little children to be the greatest in His kingdom. Have you ever observed the character of a child before the issues of life consume their hearts?

Take notice of how they trust. Children can fight with each other, and within the same hour, carry on play, as if nothing ever happened.

Children love their parents unconditionally, relying on them to make the best choices for them without worry, counting on them for their guidance and approval.

So for those who have been adopted into the family of God through the blood sacrifice of Jesus Christ, in the same unpretentious way a child loves, is the corresponding way God wants us to give and receive love: With a pure heart. When you have forgiven someone, don't assume that they should still be a part of your life.

Yes, you should forgive, but you have the right to move on thereafter. Example: Lately my kid's father has been visiting them at my home. When he's around, he sometimes displays the pain of losing me due to his actions. He becomes overwhelmingly frustrated for absolutely nothing; he gets caught up and wants to argue over the slightest thing, for example, "Why do I have the pizza slice that's slightly burnt when no one else does?" Crazy! I tell ya!

He'll act as if I told the oven to bake the pizza unevenly. Our parental relationship has the potential to become a hot mess, but thank God for the Holy Spirit. My home exudes peace and because of this, he tries to come in and disrupt the flow of things.

The tranquility within my walls can't be overlooked or even denied. There is a strong sense of order that can't be missed, and I know that bothers him. The fact that when he left, he thought I would crumble. Like the song says, "He thought I'd lie down and die," but oh not I.

As much as I would like to have a man around, this is one situation I will never return to again under any circumstances.

An angel literally would have to visit me and tell me that he is the one, and even then, I probably wouldn't accept. I am so serious. Many people couldn't understand how I could be with someone for 11 years and not have an ounce of feeling left for him.

I merely tell them that anything is possible with God. When I asked E to leave, I pretty much made it easier for him, too, because I knew he had someone else and had plans to leave anyway. But when he left, God started my healing and I never looked back.

The Book of Proverbs speaks of a dog returning to its vomit. Well, guess what? I'm not a dog plus the smell of vomit makes me sick. At times, I think my baby daddy forgets we are no longer together or is obviously in denial.

If it had not been for wisdom and understanding, out of desperation or fear of being alone, I probably would have run back to him the first opportunity I got.

But God gives us choices, and He always wants us to choose wisely.

Every doorknob obtains a keyhole, and each key made is assigned to that particular door, right? Any ol' key wouldn't be able to access entry or even fit. It must be a particular key, specifically designed to fit inside that particular hole. You'll find that some keys actually will slide inside the hole, assuming that it will unlock the door, but as you try to turn it, the lock won't budge. I said that to say this…Every penis is not made to fit perfectly into your vagina. When you were designed, there was only one crafted, for that perfect fit. There is only one that has the power to unlock your heart, that is the one that was created to become one with you. So don't settle for any ol' key.

Forgive and keep it moving; no need to get caught up!

I would rather be alone and at peace than linked up in a relationship with someone who's making me miserable.

I knew a lady who lived in my area; she was gorgeous, intelligent, humble, and hard-working. She had a beautiful home that she shared with her husband and their three teenage daughters.

This couple had been married for more than 22 years. When you would see them together, they were always holding hands or going out somewhere. They appeared to be a match made in heaven.

The way her house was positioned, if I were to look out of my bedroom window, located on the second floor of my townhome, I would be able to see right onto their back patio. There were nights when they would be sitting out on their French provincial-style patio, having a candlelit dinner, gazing into each other's eyes. Now, I was not spying or anything…. just admiring the fact that I was looking at a couple who loved each other.

I'm often amazed at how quickly we tend to judge people only by what we see and have it all wrong.

Their marriage was in shambles, just a few months after that fascinating romantic dinner I'd witnessed, the love story became an absolute catastrophe. Her husband had been cheating on her all along and was planning his exit. Plenty nights, he outright refused to come home. It had gotten so bad between the two that he did completely move out.

This poor woman was heartbroken and in need of a shoulder to lean on. I have made it my business to reach out and show support to people despite my introverted personality.

Her story is so painful, days she'd come over, her eyes would be bloodshot red due to crying all night; this is a woman who sacrificed her entire life only to be gravely betrayed by a man whom she thought she would grow old with.

As she spoke, her tears increasingly fell, her shattered heart was too much for her to bear; her misery; was uncontrollable. Her eyes remained swollen for days. During her time of grief, I would stop by her house to check on her and would sense a spirit of defeat deep down in her soul.

This was my opportunity to point to the cross, so I took advantage and ministered to the word of God, speaking life over the situation.

Sometimes God will allow us to go so low until we have nowhere else to look but up.

The unexpected breakup of this couple still saddens me to this day, because this was a marriage I believed in. To have seen them in their better times dress to impress, stepping out to paint the town red, gave me hope that marriages in this present age could still last, despite all the lunacy in the world.

This woman who I witnessed suffered so terribly but still is one of the most loving and thoughtful women I know today. I am still praying that God will restore her marriage. The statement is true "You never know what a person is going through until you know them personally". Out of all the things that I had to endure, including my faults and my failures, I can indisputably say that I have been tested and I am approved.

I know that this journey can become extensive. It's rather confusing, if you're leaning towards your understanding.

There still are days when I just want to stay in bed and not face what's ahead, especially during testing times when the Lord seems to be quiet and distant.

Most of us want to make it to the Promised Land, but just as the Lord tested the children of Israel while in the wilderness, we all must undergo hardship. If God did not put us through the fire, we could not identify with what is on the inside of us.

The funniest part about the purging process is God already knows what is in you. He may give you an exam that causes you to look at yourself.

Example: A couple of days ago, I was feeling wonderful after worshiping and praising God; my mind was crystal clear. I felt tremendously revitalized. So right after prayer, I decided to go pick up a few things from the store. While leaving the house, I had peace beyond measure subsequently after my time spent with the Lord.

Shortly, after leaving the store, some young woman who was obviously not looking where she was going came out of nowhere and flew out right in front of me, cutting me off, and totally ignoring the stop sign. I instantly became furious and held down my horn for at least 30 seconds as I trailed closely behind her. As we pulled up at the next stop, I could see her watching me in her sideview mirror. I didn't have a problem with letting her see that I was watching her as well. I continued to gaze at her with a furious stare on my face, and if looks could kill, this lady would be dead. I needed her to see I had no mercy for what she had just done by running that stop sign and cutting me off.

The stillness I'd felt fifteen minutes earlier was long gone. I allowed the devil to steal my joy, just that quick.

So you see, we are often put into difficult situations because most times this brings the authenticity out of us; our true nature... No wonder I needed a Savior.

When things are going well, and everyone around us is acting all soft and cuddly, it gives way for us to display our best behavior.

However, as soon as someone steps out of line, offends us, or things seem to be going all wrong, we become a force to be reckoned with.

Part of becoming whole is knowing your faults and admitting the truth, at least to yourself. If you never confront your issues, you can't possibly become a better person because you're living in denial. The hardest thing to do is to look at yourself in the mirror. Do you like who's staring back at you? Deceiving yourself is no way to live.

On rainy days, I enjoy making a cup of hot green tea, popping in a good movie, and then curling up with my plush robe while lying in bed. I enjoy these moments of freedom, of not having a man to answer to, of not having to wonder about what he's doing or who he's doing.

I can kick back, relax, and look like a straight-up hot mess as long as I want to. If you are single right now...Embrace it! You are free with no other obligation except to your Creator.

Some married couples wish the roles were reversed. But if you are married and regretting it, spark some intimacy by simply holding hands without speaking and gazing into each other eyes. Appreciate the fact that a lot of singles wish they were in your shoes. Be grateful for the life you have been given until the Lord gives you the desires of your heart.

He knows what he is doing, and I can assure you can put your total trust in Him.

There's this middle-aged woman who's also a member of the gym I work out at. She looks to be about in her early forties. Her body is outstanding – exotically sculpted and well-defined. She's there every day – I know this because I'm there every day as well – and while I'm walking the treadmill, I'd see her doing her thing over in the area that has the weights. I noticed the other women stare at her with admiration; I could almost read their minds.

They tend to envy her in the worst way; I know they want what she has, down to her knee bones. What I observed was some sad cases, mainly because they don't know the pain this woman is in; the hard work, the dedication, the time, and the struggle she has to go through to look like that.

It's quite simple: Little effort produces little results, no effort produces no results, and great effort produces great results.

People see the result of your life and don't realize everything essential for you to reach your goal. Every process takes time, but the more you invest, the bigger the return.

Since I have looked loneliness in the face, it has allowed me to overcome my challenges. My eyes are focused on a brighter future, the reason being, that I have decided to let go of all of the negative thoughts, issues, and baggage that was corrupting my life. I am not ashamed to say "Yes, I have struggled with a lot of things, but the greatest stronghold was loneliness." If you are expecting luck to bring you out of your trials and tribulations, then I'd say to you Good Luck.

I had to bind the word of God in my heart, tie it to my soul, and lose self-pity, thoughts of defeat, and trying to figure it all out. This is when the chains of hopelessness started to fall off. You were created to do astounding things, to exceed beyond your wildest expectations, even though life tosses you to and fro, best believe that there's a God you can count on, He holds the anchor and refuses to let go. If you trust Him without doubting Him, you will survive.

There is a vast issue many people of today do not want to face, especially when you've reached a certain level in life and people are expecting you to act in conjunction with what's been accomplished.

The American Dream! You've gained the whole world but lost so much in the process, including yourself. You realized that exchanging values for valuables didn't bring happiness, only sorrow. Sacrificing peace for persuasion only ushered in grief, sleepless nights, and a hollow shell.

Speaking of which, the last job I worked paid handsomely. I slaved at the airport as a reservationist. It was a temporary position with dreadful flexible hours. This job allowed me to clean up my credit and make a lot of other financial adjustments, but there was a problem, a huge one: I was wholly discontented. At work I would sit at my desk asking myself, "Do people do this all of their lives?" Do they religiously fall into this same routine pattern daily for years and years although it brings them no joy whatsoever? Go to work, come home, shower, eat, and then go to bed only to do it all over again. Probably not in that order but mainly this is the ritual. I wondered, when did they ever get to enjoy the fruit of their labor? Was it only on weekends or vacation time?

Now I'm not knocking hard-working people that do what they gotta do to survive, but if you're gonna do it, at least like what you do. I've seen so many people carry terrible attitudes to work and end up taking their frustration out on the customers. You'd think someone was holding a gun to their heads every day, forcing them to get up and go. Why get into a field in which you can't stand what you do?

Have you ever seen a mad nurse or an angry teacher? It is alarming. Who wants the nurse from hell to touch them? You went through all that training to do what? Work with the ill and you don't even like being around sick people? Work with kids and you don't even like kids?

I had a reality check that day. I knew right then and there I couldn't do it, that this occupation wasn't for me. So when the time came for me to become permanent, one of the managers asked if I would like to join the team. I kindly declined. After leaving the job, my experience there prompted me to dig deeper and be real with myself. It caused me to ask questions like, "What are my gifts or talents? What was I passionate about? What were some of the things I'd like to do that brought joy? The answers led my thoughts back to my childhood.

I remembered all the writing I used to do and how I loved it, whether it was a poem, or play, etc. I was zealous over the skills I possessed, and being able to recall how self-motivated I was back then allowed me to shift my focus and get back to the one thing that brought contentment.

Realizing I'd been blessed with the gift of writing at an early age was an epiphany! Or better yet, a revelation.

Hold up, I'm not suggesting that anyone should leave their careers, jobs, homes, or families. All I'm saying is; that if you are unhappy where you are, it may be time to re-evaluate your existence.

Have you ever reached a point in your life where you felt like you have given so much of yourself to others that there was nothing else left to give? Well, you are certainly not alone; the overwhelming sense of depletion is not uncommon if you are experiencing loneliness.

I remember feeling like this on my granddaughter's fifth birthday. While I was getting dressed, my strength failed, so I lay on the bed and started shedding tears. I didn't know what was wrong, so I called on the Lord for help.

Anybody in this state can easily fly off the deep end, if they never reach out for help. Your body can keep going even while your heart is telling you, you've had enough. Listen to your heart. I'd been so wrapped up in doing things for others, and at the same time, neglecting myself. When going through periods of off-and-on sadness, Stop! And call it like it is; an issue.

Finding Peace

One other necessity loneliness will try to rob you of is your peace. It keeps you focused on things you don't have rather than being grateful for the things that you do have.

Most people whom I've spoken with throughout my lifetime seemed to be struggling with some sort of melancholy spirit. I realized most if not all, were full of anxieties and/or worries of some sort. Whether it be about the future, where they would end up financially, or how they are going to pay their next bill, worrying will put so much stress on your life and you can't add a single hour to it. Stressing over something is not going to change anything.

Inner harmony should be a constant flow if you are walking in the Spirit; meaning, you are walking in complete love.

When my first child was a newborn, the love I felt looking into her eyes for the first time was out of this world. I couldn't believe that I was holding a piece of me in my arms. The moment was beautiful, but my love had limits. For this reason, the love I had for her when she was a baby was constantly growing as she got older.

Every day it seemed as though I could love her more and more. The love I had for her had increased over the years. By the time she was fifteen, you would think I couldn't love her anymore, but I could. She is grown now, and still, my love for her continues to grow.

We as humans love this way, with limits. On the other hand, God's love for us is uniquely different. His love is limitless.

He cannot love us any more than He already does. Why? Because He is love, He doesn't change in nature or character.

On our good and bad days, His love remains the same, even when He is applying judgment.

Moreover, to love like this, we must first come to the full knowledge of Christ and the love He had for us on the cross.

This is the total fullness of who God is, which will allow our love for others to be complete. Christ fulfilled the law when he died on the cross for our sins; we fulfill the law of Christ when we walk in an all-inclusive love.

I remember reading the story of Jacob in the Bible. He loved Rachael; she was beautiful, her body was banging, and it was an instantaneous love-at-first-sight ordeal. On the other hand, he rejected his wife Leah. She wasn't as attractive as her sister Rachael, but Leah had a heart of gold. She did everything she could to appease her husband but remained unloved by him. This story alone should open up female eyes. Leah was like some women today. She thought having a child would keep Jacob; she thought by giving birth to all his sons, that he would realize the prize he had.

Even though Leah lacked beauty, she was on a never-ending quest to be recognized by him.

After reading the entire story, I remember telling the Lord how I never wanted to end up as some man's Leah. Months went by, and what seemed to be this sad story was brought back to my remembrance; suddenly the Holy Spirit was shining a light on Leah's situation.

Although Jacob overlooked Leah, she was captivating to God.

Yes, he deserted, denied, and rejected her, but the Lord comforted, embraced, and accepted her.

Eventually, Leah gave up her quest in trying to get a man to love her and looked to a God who saw beauty in her. Leah became whole by acknowledging God's love for her. My views of a dire ending completely shifted.

While breaking your neck, doing back flips, and jumping over tables for a man, you could be investing all that energy in a relationship with someone who cares. Jesus!

Submitting and surrendering to His will enables us to be imparted with His Spirit and gives room for the Holy Spirit to teach us how to truly love. We then can rest assured that we will experience a peace that surpasses all understanding.

* * *

I would say that I'm somewhat of a pacifist. I believe there are numerous ways to handle certain situations without all the drama and quarreling, and if you pay attention to the reason we as humans argue, throw fits, or fight, you'll find the root of discontentment.

In other words, in Pride, you can't have what you want so you throw temper tantrums. You are never too old to right your wrongs if you have fallen into this category.

I constantly and relentlessly remind myself to keep my eyes on Jesus. Like in the vision, when my focus starts shifting, I'm more likely distracted by things around me, that's when the rising waters and winds of life seem to drown my faith and blow me into despair.

During the fourth watch of the night, Jesus went out to them, walking on the lake. When the disciples saw him walking on the lake, they were terrified. "It's a ghost," they said and cried out in fear. But Jesus immediately said to them, "Take courage! It is I. Don't be afraid."

"Lord if it's you," Peter replied, "Tell me to come to you on the water." "Come," he said. Then Peter got out of the boat, walked on water, and came toward Jesus. But when he saw the wind, he was afraid and, beginning to sink, cried out, "Lord save me!"

Immediately Jesus reached out his hand and caught him. "You of little faith," he said, "why did you doubt?" (Matthew 14:22)

In addition, this is an example of our lives when we start doubting or allowing this world to engross us.

We start sinking! As a young girl riddled with major insecurities, I'm still working on things about myself to this day that I'm not proud of.

There are segments of my life that I still need to confront, areas I know about myself that would be unbearable for a man to deal with. So I must continue to grow and not become complacent in my walk with Christ.

My tolerance for ignorance is extremely low, and I tend to shy away from people who are indifferent and things that I don't completely understand. Self-absorption is the gorilla in the room. Point blank: If I do not feel it, then I am not with it.

I agree that every one of us needs to do an internal self-examination.

Recently, I was scrolling Facebook and ran across a post that read, "If you're not perfect, then please don't Judge me." It reminded me of when Jesus spoke to those religious folk and said, "Let him that is without sin cast the first stone."

I run into all kinds of believers, but in my opinion, the self-righteous ones are by far the worst. The reason I know this is because I used to be one of them. I was dreadfully judgmental and outright hypocritical most of the time. Like many, you can see their religion but you can't find their love. The Holy Spirit revealed that my heart was in danger of becoming pure stone, moreover waxed cold, if I didn't repent because I lacked compassion and understanding of my weaker brothers and sisters in Christ.

There I was, standing before God, praying and asking Him to send my mate and deliver me from the sufferings of loneliness, and at the same time refusing to comfort my fellow man.

I was back to my old habits of leaning on my understanding. I took the correction with joy and allowed to correct my mistakes.

God then cleansed me and replaced my heart of stone with a heart of flesh. He exchanged His beauty for my ashes.

They will return to it and remove all its vile images and detestable idols. I will give them an undivided heart and put a new spirit in them; I will remove from them the heart of stone and give them a heart of flesh. Then they will follow my decrees and be careful to keep my laws. They will be my people and I will be their God. (Ezekiel 11:18

As you can see, God is telling us to turn back to him. You must be a willing spirit for this to occur. The Lord will never impose His will on anyone. Submit to His will, and He will use you abundantly.

After my grandmother died, I couldn't understand how God would get the glory out of something so devastating. Many nights I'd lay in the bed crying, and never once did I try to see God's plan in it. I'd ask Him "Why now? Why did she have to leave me now?" I'd asked this a few times in my suffering, and eventually, He gave me the answer – well, not exactly an answer but more like a question.

God asked me, "If I had given her ten more years, would that have made a difference in the way you are feeling right now?" Then He asked, "What if I would have given her twenty more years, would a longer life have mattered in the end, wouldn't you still have sorrow?"

His questions brought clarity; later dawned on me that if I could have had it my way, my grandma would have never died, which meant I was being unreasonable. Her appointed time to depart this earth came and I needed to continue to trust that He would heal my brokenness. God, in all his wisdom, turned the questions I had on my heart back to me, so that I could acknowledge the questions that I was asking, followed by the answer. We were all born to leave this earth, and trying to figure out why didn't make sense because if she had lived 50 more years, nothing could change the way I would inevitably feel about her death, since I loved her so much. So asking Him a question like "Why now?" was irrelevant. He is ingenious. My grandmamma was blessed with a long life and I was granted thirty-five years to be a part of it.

Rather than keep me in a state of despair, He chose to use this vessel and turn my pain into passion. He placed in me an ability to reach other smokers by sharing a testimony about my grandmother's affliction in her last days here on earth. My heart goes out to people who I see puffing on a cigarette.

My grandma was a habitual smoker, and even though she had quit six years before dying, the damage was already done. Funny as it may sound, sharing this with others helped me heal. Staying busy can play a major role in your happiness. Sitting around sulking and thinking about crap you want and don't have consumes you. It deprives you of your peace. Try focusing on mind, body, and spirit.

I told you, I joined a gym, changed my eating habits, and transformed my body in a matter of months. The yearlong contract with a local gym motivated me to stay dedicated, and it worked. Within three months of that time, working out was part of my regimen; it later became my lifestyle.

This goes out to all my singles out there waiting on God to bless them with a mate. Is it possible for you to find someone who will love you unconditionally? Of course. The question is: Will you be ok with it, in the state that you're in? Honest question: Are you pleased with your appearance right now? If you are, then the next paragraph may not apply to you on a physical aspect, but it may if you're already married. There are plenty of people who are married to a remarkable person and their insecurities are tearing down the marriage.

Women: You can spot a beautiful woman in the room before he does. Next, you zoom in on him to make sure his eyes don't wander, and if he happens to glance in her direction, oh boy! The gloves come off, all hell breaks loose.

Making small adjustments to your lifestyle is not solely for him, but as you can see, for you. When you are fit and healthy you feel less burdened with insecurities because you discern on the inside, you look just as good as the next woman. SO TAKE HEED, SINGLES!

Before God brings you to that special person, WORK ON YOU!

You'll then, not only have a mate that loves you unconditionally but you'll also be able to stand with the best of them in confidence. Finding love is a beautiful thing, however negative thoughts you may have about yourself can hinder the flow of that beauty.

Why not exude everything the word love stands for? God in His entire splendor taught me how to love and showed me the meaning of my existence ultimately giving me purpose and restoring my hope. His unfailing love is a shoulder that I never had; to cry on. While the trials in my life caused my heart to bleed, His protection and compassion healed and offered security in ways I could not comprehend.

Spots in my life where it was cold, but His touch was warm. My hard negative thoughts softened with His words. My emptiness is filled with His presence. We became intimate; He will forever be the lover of my soul.

I can say that by His strength, I continue to shine like the name in which He gave me many years ago, "STAR." The Lord changed my name y'all.

I surely didn't. I was embedded in sorrow, too defeated to ever think that I was some sort of Star. But God!

He saw things in me before the foundation of the world. If you ever need proof that God knows you inside out, then here it is:

O Lord, you have searched me and you know me. You know when I sit and when I rise; you perceive my thoughts from afar. You discern my going out and my lying down; you are familiar with all my ways. Before a word is on my tongue, you know it completely, O Lord. You hem me in behind and before; you have laid your hand upon me, too lofty for me to attain. Where can I go from your Spirit? Where can I flee from your presence? (Psalms 139:1)

From this verse alone, you should at least have an idea about God's knowledge concerning you. Don't get caught up in the acceptance of people. You would be surprised at how many friends you DO NOT have, once you start moving past their expectations.

By God changing my name to Star, this alone has left a stench in people's nostrils. Best believe not everyone is rooting for me, and more surprisingly the ones I thought were riding for me, appear to act rather strange. It's funny when a few of them will say to me, "Don't get too skinny now." What in the heck does that mean? (I'm trying to keep the writings in this book PG by it being a part of Kingdom work). But as I was saying, don't be alarmed when the ones who knew the most about your adversities appear to be the ones who despise your success all the more.

Fake people come to a dime a dozen, and they only wanna hear from you when things are going wrong, just to stay all up in your business. The word of God refers to them as busybodies. Don't let these folk discourage you. Some of my friendships I ended up letting go of because they were especially toxic.

I found myself in a position where I'd always have to lick the person's wounds, even if it wasn't my fault. Always on the brink of almost apologizing for what God was doing in my life.

If we went to the mall together, they were uncomfortable.

If I mentioned how well my kids were doing in school, they also seemed uneasy.

It was so tiresome of forever having to appease this individual in the friendship; I seemed to have always pushed their "easily offended button." I have met my share of females who be on some competition bull crap when I didn't have a clue they had signed me up for the game.

Another thing I can't stand is pettiness. That is my ultimate pet peeve. There was an incident that happened a few years back that caused a big riff in one of my friendships. This person and I hadn't spoken in over two years, and out of the blue, she called me one day. I did not have a problem with her calling, but all she wanted to do was nitpick at the past. To keep it completely real, I had done nothing to this girl, but she insisted that I did. When I asked her to bring clarity as to what I had done to her, she got quiet, having nothing to say. She would occasionally laugh while explaining herself, which put in the mind frame that this person was on assignment by satan. The conversation was just that confusing. By the way, she was carrying on about nothing; anyone listening would have assumed that I had recently spoken with her. But two years had passed, and sadly she was still stuck in that same mindset, that same old pettiness that tore the friendship down to begin with. I was so over it, all I could do was shake my head. I had no desire to rekindle anything. Right then and there I knew that I didn't miss out on nothing; but drama.

Since I've evolved, I tend to observe things in another light. If you don't like a person, don't hang around them. It's just that simple. When we fail to check ourselves, we deceive ourselves. Calling someone a hater when you know in your heart that you too are an undercover hater makes you a real fake, a hypocrite.

One thing I will never do is try to explain why God is blessing me. I'm sorry if a person feels awkward around me, but just like a leopard can't change his spots, I can't change my God and I surely can't change his mind concerning me.

If you have someone in your circle praying for your fall, drop 'um. Trying to keep dysfunctional people around just because you feel sorry for them can get you killed; I know that's a hard truth. I've never really been the type to try and sugarcoat anything. It is what it is.

Check out the story of Lot's wife in the Bible. When they were leaving Sodom, the Angel gave her specific instructions not to look back. She disobeyed and what happened? She was destroyed.

Unfortunately, there are things we must let go of, and never return to.

If a person is not encouraging you, edifying you, or at least praying for you, cut them off. You were called to be a good friend, mother, father, husband, wife, brother, sister, etc., you were not called to be the Holy Spirit.

Allow God to work on the person, and if their future is in your cards, maybe y'all will hook up again one day. If not, that's cool, continue to pray for them.

A rear-view mirror is just what it says it is. It's supposed to be small because you should only be able to glance at it while you're moving ahead. Now the windshield is much larger for the reason that it gives you a bigger picture. That's the one you should keep your eyes on.

Forcing relationships makes no sense at all. It may do more damage than good.

You are on a quest for restoration, security, and serenity. It's coming from a place where no one in this world can give.

I appreciate everything I have gone through. If I had not encountered these hardships, hurdles, and setbacks, where would my faith be right now? I would crumble under the slightest sign of pressure, adversity, or shortcomings, solely relying on things that I can see, things I can hear, things I can touch, which in reality is no Faith at all.

Faith is the substance of things hoped for, the evidence of things unseen.

(Hebrews 11:1)

There is a spiritual side of you that many disregard. If this fraction of itself is neglected, it starves. Three parts make up who you are. They are the soul, the body, and the spirit, and all need to be maintained to function properly, because when – not if but when – situations around you start to unravel, you come apart as well because there is no foundation.

You can go to church seven days a week, sing in the choir, shout, scream, and yell until your tonsils fall out, but where there is no word, there is no water, where there is no water, there is no root, if there is no root, nothing can flourish.

Therefore, everyone who hears these words of mine and puts them into practice is like a wise man who built his house on the rock. The rains came down and the streams rose, and the winds blew and beat against that house yet it did not fall because it had its foundation on the rock. (Matthew 7:24)

If you haven't picked up the word of God in a while and you suddenly feel desolation buried down in your soul; one of the causes may be that you are grieving the Holy Spirit. God gives His Spirit to every believer who chooses to believe and live for Him. The treasure that God has placed in you thrives off His word. He counsels by referencing the word of God. So if you seldom pick up the word, how would His Spirit be able to bring anything you've read back to your remembrance? You are activating with little power, then again no power at all. By obeying your feelings, you somehow feed the flesh, however obeying the word of God, feeds the Spirit.

This is the reason why strongholds may still be holding you. A stronghold can be the spirit of oppression, lust, addiction, greed, or adultery. There are many forms. So whatever your struggle may be, if you have been stuck in that thing way too long, you may lack God's strength. Only by accepting His power, then are we able to walk the way Christ walked, not by our works or by might.

There is no way I can please God with my efforts, I alone cannot stand in the face of temptation and consistently reject it, without the Holy Spirit's help. My stronghold was lust. I ached for a man, and as hard as I tried to conquer these desires on my own, the more I failed.

If you're anything like me, then you know that the spirit of lust is serious, that IT IS NO JOKE. Certain TV shows, music, especially old slow love songs, and explicit sensual images also can ignite these sex demons. When I'm armored up, I'm unstoppable, but as soon as I start slipping if the wind blows too hard on the wrong body part, then I might have a problem!

This is for anyone who thinks they can wrestle and take down immorality by themselves. Point blank, you will not be successful.

Pointing the finger is especially humorous to me. We want to blame God when we get ourselves into this crazy state of affairs, by handling stuff backward a lot of the time; stepping out on our own, then when it all goes wrong, later asking Him to bless our mess.

For example, let's say you want to start a business. You secure all the necessary measures to ensure you will run a prosperous company.

Later, the business fails due to whatever reason; never realizing that if you had consulted with God in the beginning, this may not have happened.

So the business or marriage etc. goes down the drain, then we want to blame God for our downfall, and He is sitting back like, "I never cosigned that, to begin with."

Adam of the Bible was a blame shifter. And we can find ourselves in this same kind of predicament, too, if we choose to do things our way.

There's a way that seems right to a man but in the end, leads to destruction.

(Proverbs 16:25)

I was online reading different blogs and I ran across one that said, "Waiting on God." After reading, I came across this one comment and was appalled. It read:

I'm a Christian virgin, I go to church faithfully. I have never had a man because I thought God would bless me with an excellent godly Christian man. But No! He gives me someone and lets them mishandle me, some God. I pray and pray for a good husband only to have God mistreat me. This guy has been mistreating me and putting me through stuff my entire life just because I don't look the way God wants me to look. How wrong is that? I pray and pray and pray to God, and he ignores me because I didn't make the same mistakes as others, I'm not a slut and I never will be one, just to get a blessing from him. I'm educated. I'm also a good quality person. What more does he want from me? I'm now 34 years old and he skips over me. I lost my whole family, everyone I was close to. I have no one to turn to and God won't bless me with an excellent godly husband. People tell me all the time that no one wants me and this is the reason I'm still single. And God looks over me just because I'm not a hooker. Everyone, please stop bragging about a blessing that others don't have. Spread the good news but don't boast about it, because look at all the mistakes you made to get married. I have been praying for years and trying to do all the right things and get looked over because I'm not a whore nor am I pretty. You are wrong for bragging about being married because if the shoe was on the other foot, you would hate it.

Was this as confusing to you as it was to me? I doubt it! See what I mean by blame-shifting. Be very careful with that. As I was reading this, I honestly did have a lot of pity for this person. It's obvious she has been deceived and is riddled with all kinds of emotional chaos and insecurities. Let's dissect this letter line by line for a moment.

First thing first, let's start by recognizing that this person is lonely:

1. She says she's a "Christian virgin that goes to church faithfully" (She never mentions a relationship with Christ).

2. "She's never been with a man because she thought God would bless her with an excellent godly husband" (There are two things wrong here; not only did she lean on her understanding, but her reasons for holding out on being with a man are all wrong).

3. "But No! He gives me someone and lets them mishandle me. Some God" (As you see here, blame-shifting and anger become relevant.).

4. "I pray and pray for a husband, only to have God mistreat me" (Here, she starts accusing God.).

5. "This guy has been mistreating me and putting me through stuff my entire life just because I don't look the way God wants me to look, how wrong is that? I pray and pray and pray to God and he ignores me because I didn't make the same mistakes as others" (I wish I could break this one down, but I'm utterly confused.).

6. "I'm not a slut and will never be one just to get blessings from him I'm educated, and I'm also a good quality person." (Can you sense some self-righteousness?)

7. "What more does he want from me? I'm thirty-four years old now, and he skips over me" (This pride, or feeling as though God owes her something.).

8. "I lost my whole family, everyone I was close to, I have no one to turn to and God won't bless me with an excellent godly husband" (self-pity).

9. "People tell me all the time that no one wants me and this is the reason that I'm single. And God overlooks me just because I'm not a hooker" (She is being deceived by satan here.).

10. "Everyone please stop bragging about blessings that others don't have, spread the good news but don't boast about it, because look at all the mistakes you made just to be married" (Here she proceeds to lash out and take her frustrations out on others.).

11. "I have been praying for years and trying to do all the right things, and get overlooked because I'm not a whore nor am I pretty." (She is trying to impose guilt on her readers).

12. "You are wrong for bragging about being married because if the shoe was on the other foot, you would hate it" (To sum it up, no relationship with God is found here. And if you are a man reading this, would you marry someone with this type of mindset?).

Don't get me wrong, my heart goes out to this woman and her situation. But so much negativity can take place when the motives of your heart are not right. This woman is fixated on claiming that she's this good person. And from this comment, I can see why God holds off on giving us things so that He can test us. I'm no judge, but by what you just read, would you say this person failed or passed the test?

You will get nowhere by blaming God for anything, He is just; He is blameless; there is no wrong in Him whatsoever. Your world can be crumbling down around you, you could have had a lifetime of ugly things happen to you, but that does not take away from the fact that God is good. Even when He is punishing or judging us, His character remains the same. A lion cannot become a zebra nor can a bear become a monkey. God does not change in nature, He is who He is, and He is good all of the time. She mentioned God gave her a person who mistreats her. What on earth makes her feel like God had anything to do with that? Using your good works to try and pawn Him out of a blessing is an outrage. Pride can seep into a person's heart and have them believe that they are good and deserving of all great things.

And what does being a whore mean to a Holy God? Tell me, how does being a hooker and getting a blessing fall into play? I'm lost! I tell you the truth: By not taking the time out to get to know Him, we can easily get it so twisted and a lot of us have the wrong perception as to who Yahweh is.

So we carry this rage in our hearts directed toward Him. Are you in danger of this?

She claims she does not have anyone, but what about the God she's been praying to all of these years? Isn't He her present help in a time of trouble? See, when we neglect a relationship with Him and start overly catering to a church and trying to be good within our own efforts as you can see, you will flop.

God is not impressed with how good you can be, He's primarily concerned with the relationship you have with His Son, and putting all of your security in Him.

Please understand that your works will not get you into Heaven. Homegirl thought her work was gonna land her a man and not just any man but "an excellent man." Whoa! I feel her pain, I know what is to wait and wait for something, but to blame God for your shortcomings is a no-no. And if you're thinking another person is going to solve all your problems in life…Whew, think again. If you are a person who is also waiting for marriage, why do you even want to be married? Did you know; the institution of marriage was set up by God to demonstrate Christ's love for His bride? (Which is the church, adding together to bring sanctified children into the world, to saturate the earth?) So if you are looking forward to it, just to make you happy or to have guiltless sex, look again dear friends. Marriage is a ministry, and happiness starts with you. A person should only be able to add to the happiness already there.

If you are not happy with yourself, how can you expect someone else to be happy with you? In all actuality, you will eventually end up less cheerful if you are constantly relying on people to make you blissful.

When I first became a Christian, I followed signs; now that I'm more mature and have a better understanding, signs now follow me.

When I began my walk with the Lord, I honestly didn't know what to expect. I guess I thought every hour would be happy hour. Now, I comprehend that every trial, every test or mess, was mandatory. For us to have a more solid friendship with Him, we must endure quite a few hardships.

This is a covenant relationship I'm in; a covenant means an agreement where two parties are involved. Some believers think they are in a one-sided relationship with Christ and feel like they don't have to hold down their end of the bargain.

Well, let me say this: The blessings that God speaks about in His word are for those who are in covenant.

Stop thinking because so and so just bought a new house or car that they are automatically blessed. I'm not saying they're not, but satan allows you to obtain gifts, too. Matter of fact, he'll give you everything this world has to offer.

But the things he cannot give you are love, joy, peace, forbearance, kindness, self-control, gentleness, goodness, or faithfulness.

The devil may give you abundance in material wealth, but abundant life he will and cannot give you.

As with any friendship, my relationship with Jesus in some seasons seems to be a little distant. However, He is always consistent, and His stature never changes. I still find myself at times not wanting to read the word, not in the mood to worship or pray, even so, when we are faithless, God is still faithful. I briefly explained the covenant; this contract, this agreement between us, signed with His Son's blood. I'm up and down on some days. Nonetheless, He remains the same, every single day.

God pursued me; this is how a part of His love demonstrates. He illustrated His concern for me by never giving up on me. If you want to know how much a man desires you, he'll show you in his pursuit. It was obvious that my earthly father had no interest in getting to know me. His actions showed; He didn't have an ounce of care.

Ladies, if you're in a relationship and you're doing the chasing, please give up! If a man wants you, you'd know it.

I'm so tired of seeing these queens break dancing for these drop shots. We as women are worth so much more than to have a man degrade us. But we gotta know this.

Why are we lowering our standards for a man and in our hearts, we know that he could care less about us? Some of these women have made half of these men lazy by giving the treasure box away so easily. Some men don't believe in pursuing women anymore because a lot of them (not all) would rather settle for the easier route and shack up with a female who is willing to give up all her milk, without putting up a fight.

Whatever happened to a man opening up the car door for you? Or going out on a date; he pays the bill, and expects nothing in return? Has it gotten so bad as to where we chase them down now? We blow up their phones and then proceed to act out of character when he doesn't cater to our wants for a deeper commitment. Why expect more now, than he was willing to give at the beginning of the relationship?

I can't wrap my head around, half of the foolishness I see online. It's shocking to see what a person would do for a few likes. If you are sleeping around with different men, stop it! HIV is running more rampant now than back in the day. If you are lying down unprotected with different men today, you may wake up with something you can't get rid of tomorrow. The wages of sin is death, and even though you will or have already accepted Christ, remember we must still pay for our actions. God's forgiveness is for everyone who asks, but the consequences of our actions are inevitable. When I asked God to forgive my sins, He did; however, He didn't take away my children.

They are a product of my sin, so don't think that just because you have been forgiven, certain things will automatically disappear.

The good news in all is, that all things work together for good for those who love the Lord.

Don't get me wrong, I have nothing against anyone who has HIV. I'm humble enough to acknowledge that it could have been me. My birth mom happens to be infected. From what I'm told, she has been a carrier for around twenty years or so. A life of partying, drinking, and promiscuity in her younger days caught up with her. The things you do in the past and present can affect your future. Although we never had much of a relationship, I still want the best for her. I'll call every once in a while to see how she's doing or give her a ride to the store just to spend time with her.

I have forgiven her for every single thing she's done to me. I hold no grudge against her because I understand now that most of it was completely out of her control. Nevertheless, is it possible to love someone I never knew? When I look into her eyes; I see a stranger, even though the mother I'd always hoped for is trapped somewhere within her, I can never find that woman. Mental illness is serious, and she has been living with this condition ever since she was a teenager. She now takes her medication without putting up a scuffle because she is no longer in denial about her sickness and because she has given her life to Christ, despite all the physical ailments she may possess, she is freer than she ever will be. She's in a place in her life where she too has looked loneliness in the face. All I can say is "Good for her."

I can't wait for my baby brother to come to grips with his illness as well. He was diagnosed with the same condition our mom has, back when he was around eighteen. He was diagnosed schizophrenic while locked up and is 34 years old now. His report said that he attempted to set his jail cell on fire. My brother has been in and out of jail ever since the age of thirteen. He writes me letters often; most of them I don't quite understand, due to his penmanship. From what I can read, he thinks that he is Tupac, literally; moreover, he throws piss and feces on the prison guards, and he tells his social worker stories about him growing up in Japan. Our family has never been to Japan. The last time I went to visit him in jail, I explained how important taking his medication is, but just as our mother was in the beginning, he does not feel a need to. In his psyche, he thinks he is fully sane.

This may sound harsh, but he is safer locked up, than out here on these streets. The occurrences the last time he was out would have landed him a bullet in the head. Throwing hot coffee on unknown females, dancing in the middle of the street as cars were passing by, sitting behind people and bee–boppin' while spitting on them in public places, punching people in the face that wouldn't give him a dollar if he'd asked.

These incidents alone could have gotten him killed; by the grace of God, he is still alive. He has offended a lot of folks; furthermore, none of them knew he had a mental problem because he looks perfectly fine. My brother is tatted up with a mouth full of gold teeth, and he loves to dress. When he was free, he walked around being a menace, without intention.

Everyone in this life will reach a breaking point. I don't care how raw you think you are, or how much money you have, you will reach a crossroads in life. But the minute you realize that you can't walk this road alone, the sooner help will arrive. If satan has tricked you and got you thinking, "I got this" (alone), then you are living a lie.

Whatever has caused your loneliness, your depression, your hopelessness, your despondency; this is an issue that needs to be addressed.

When my oldest daughter started to act out in her teenage years, I brushed it off as normal rebellion, teenage hormones to say the least. My grandma, on the other hand, thought it was another case of crazies because of what she had gone through with my mother and brother.

But I wasn't convinced. I knew there was an issue, but not one reminiscent of my mom's or brother's.

Years later, a lot of energy poured into renewing me and my daughter's relationship, finally led me to the root of her dilemma. She shared some things with me that would put my entire existence on edge. When I learned of this, I was distraught and speechless.

I would love to go into detail about it, however my relationship with my kids is far more important to me than the dollar sign. I will tell you that I was beyond hurt; the pain struck me to the core, and I was completely shattered.

I was covered in so much guilt that I was suffocating in it. I went to bed enduring a nightmare and woke up within a nightmare. How could I have let something so harmful take place in my child's life and not even have a clue about it? WOW! I blamed myself, and consequently, I wouldn't forgive myself.

Forgiving others, no matter what they had done to me seemed so natural because it was so easy for me to do, but forgiving myself was a different story. This was another mountain, one so big I couldn't see on the other side of it. I felt I had failed my child as a mother. The thought of her misery haunted me so badly, day after day. I held myself responsible for everything that she had ever gone wrong in her life.

This goes to all parents who have a child who's acting out: Take time and get to the root of their crisis. It may be more serious than you think, especially if rage is involved. Don't try to figure it out on your own; talk with your children. Most kids' bad actions are a result of some hurt they may be going through or have gone through. More than a few seek attention by doing the outrageous for recognition; to compensate for the affection they have never received.

As for me, time has passed; about four years since I learned of this heartbreak, and I'm continually coping and allowing the Lord to work me through it.

Discovering Abundant Life

I'm much older now in Christ, but I'm aware that I am still a work undone. I'm also still waiting for many of God's promises to manifest in my life. The waiting part, no lie, is such a struggle. And yet I rejoice in the glory of God.

Not only so we also rejoice in our sufferings, because we know that suffering produces perseverance, perseverance, character; and character, hope and hope do not disappoint us because God has poured out his love into our hearts by the Holy Spirit, whom he has given us. (Romans 5:3)

On the other hand, what do you do when you've prayed, waited, prayed, then waited some more? What happens when you get to that place in your spirit when you feel like God has forgotten about you? When you look up and everyone around you is been blessed, when you have prayed for something, only to have another one receive it? How do you cope, when the wait becomes months, months become years, and years turn into more years? What do you do when you cry out in anguish, only to receive silence in return? What happens when you feel abandoned by God? Ignored, lost, downcasted.

As much as I love the Lord I too have experienced all these, and have asked the same questions.

Let me shed light on your situation. You are not forgotten, and it does not matter how much you kick and scream, nothing is going to happen before it's time. Your temper tantrums do not move God, but the power of prayer does, faith does. Keep in mind that God is the sovereign Father of time, and until He chooses to release your blessing(s), all you can do is wait. Look on the bright side:

Let us not become weary in doing well, for at the proper time we will reap a harvest if we do not give up. (Galatians 6:9)

So what exactly do you do again? You keep on believing, you continue to pray and be faithful. You praise God amid everything that's going on in your life. Most importantly, you keep the faith. Your breakthrough may be scheduled for tomorrow at 2:15 pm. You just never know and I'll assure you again, that you are not forgotten. God has seen all of your tears, your heartache, your faithfulness and He promises that you will not be put to shame.

If you have prayed and it seems as though God is not listening; sin can interfere with our reception to God. This is why repentance and seeking His face are particularly imperative.

At the beginning of becoming a believer, God gave me so much attention, He pacified and attended to my every whimper. I'm talking about major signs and wonders all around me. His presence remained strong in my life when I was a baby Christian, not saying He's not here now but things have changed a bit. I'm not a baby anymore, so I can't expect him to rub my aches every time I decide to have a tantrum; I'm a mature Christian now. And even though at times, I want to go back to the beginning stage food; He knows that will only hinder my walk, my love, my growth. What can a grown woman benefit from baby food? Absolutely nothing.

When I was a child, I talked like a child; I thought like a child, I reasoned like a child. When I became a man (grown), I put childish ways behind me.

(Corinthians 14:11)

We must continue to grow in our faith, if we commence to stay in one spot, we'll stop learning, stop maturing, and will eventually lose our saltiness. It's ok to press harder into God when your confidence in Him feels like it's on the rocks. It's ok to share exactly what you're going through with the One who knows you better than you know yourself. Just be real with Him, and you will develop a strong well-secured relationship. God is not interested in where you worship, He is concerned with how you worship; which must be in "Spirit and in Truth." Did you stop to ask the Lord for His Holy Spirit after you had repented?

The abundant life that we yearn for can be found, only in Him. Get a hold of all that God has promised you. For a long time, I repeated what others said about God. When folks used to quote clichés such as "God does for those that do for themselves" or "God is a God of a second chance," I was the first to say Amen. But as I grew to know Him for myself, the things I used to hear and had agreed upon at that time, a lot of it I found to be untrue. First of all, God does more for those who can't do for themselves, those who rely solely on him to provide their every need tend to be in a better place than those who put their trust in themselves. Secondly, God is a God of not just second chances, but many chances. If He were a God of only second chances, we would be dead or in hell right now.

Getting to know Him on your own will play a debt in part, entirely on your belief system. A man is what he thinks, so if you think God is against you in some way, this is how you will end up living your life. Jesus also asked Peter "Who do others say I am?" Then He went on and asked, "Who do you say I AM?" The relationship we have with Him means everything to Him. Not Religion! The revelation He gives to us about Him through His word and by His Spirit sets the course that allows us to live a healthy, full, abundant life in Him. Your spiritual well-being should never be predicated on what someone else has told you.

There are too many teachings out there for one to rely on another's thoughts and views about Christ.

As for you, the anointing you received from him remains in you, and you do not need anyone to teach you. But as his anointing teaches you about all things and as that anointing is real, not counterfeit-remain in him. (1 John 2:27)

I can't start to tell you how much joy I have now, how refreshed I feel daily, the level of peace I am experiencing, and yes I am still single. I, too, am happy to be me, and for a long time, I could not say that. I thought all these things were out of my reach.

When prosperity and goodness were spoken, I considered that word was always meant for someone else, but I am living it, and I wouldn't change it for the world. When God stripped me of everything, I then realized that I didn't need all that I thought I did. Everything we need is in Him; He shall supply all of our needs according to His riches in glory. To know that God has plans for me, to not harm me, and to give me hope and a future offers up the strength for me to persevere. And for those reading this that have never known Him, you've tried everything this world has to offer; now it's time to try Him. Taste and see that the Lord is good.

If you grew up fatherless like myself or have had a rocky relationship with him, you may experience a difficult time in differentiating God from your earthly father especially if you were subjected to abandonment and/or abuse. It may seem a bit tough to put all of your trust in someone carrying the title of father. Well, let me restore confidence since your earthly father can't even measure you to your Heavenly Father. Your Heavenly Father is the reason why you are breathing right now. He has all the power and is extremely capable of making a way out of no way. Believe me, I know better than any other, what it feels like to be neglected by a man, to feel disposed of; unwanted. Yet, as I grew in my relationship with God, all of my insecurities seemed to start falling off, but I will say that it was a process, that depends on what you want.

Do you desire a little of Him or a lot of Him? This measurement is determined by your faith, prayer, and what you are hoping for. As I grew, not having an earthly father influenced much of my relationship with men negatively, in turn, this altered how I trusted people. Contrarily, when God entered my life, He not only had to teach me how to love, but He also had to teach me how to trust. Those two things go hand in hand. You can't have love without trust, so how could I love God without trusting Him? It is impossible. Some components make up any healthy connection, these two go hand in hand, and both must be in place.

Now, when difficult seasons arise in my life, I easily can stand on the promises of God securely, only because I trust Him. You need to be planted securely for when the ground around you starts collapsing; your foundation allows you to stand strong despite the many trials and tribulations you may face. I learned that my heart is only troubled when I don't allow the Prince of Peace to come in; when I've allowed the situation to outweigh my God. In any event, the goal of our faith is to persevere, and that is going to be dreadfully hard if you don't even know the One who is a present help in times of trouble. How hard would it be for those of you who have kids, to leave your child with a stranger or someone you just met? I'm assuming you'd probably struggle with it or would never do something like that.

But, how easy would it be to leave your child with someone you've gotten to know over time who has proved they're trustworthy and that you've built something solid with? The task of leaving your child then becomes less stressful. From that analogy, you can see why getting a deeper understanding of Christ is crucial for your walk. Don't allow satan to allow you to take this lightly. Satan does not mind you going to church, singing, shouting, or using any of your gifts, but he does care about your relationship status with your Creator, and he will stop at nothing to hinder it. Just think about how many times you said that you were going to get serious with the Lord and got distracted. Something always seems to come up when you decide to get it right.

Many will say to me in that day, Lord, Lord, have we not prophesied in thy name? And in thy name have cast out devils? And in thy name done many wonderful works? And then He shall say to them: I never knew you, depart from me, ye that work iniquity. (Matthew 7:23)

Now take a moment to ponder a second on this verse in which God says, "I never knew you." What does He mean by this? When you analyze the scripture, the word makes power in His name evident, and these people were using it to perform miracles, heal the sick, etc. so yes, they knew the authority they could use to drive out demons in His name, but how much time were they spending on getting to know the One who has all power. It's almost like using your neighbor's water hose without ever really getting to know them. How awkward is that? It's basically, robbing them. To continue to use someone's things without any intention of ever getting to know the individual is outright disrespectful as well.

God's use of the term workers of iniquity perfectly suits them. Too many people only know Jesus as Savior, but only a few have made Him Lord over their lives. They wade in the shallow waters of their faith, never really learning how to swim. Those of us in Christ ought to realize how blessed we truly are. Your identity is who you are in Him. Jesus chose us while we were still in bondage; He loved us, even while sin had engulfed us. So you must serve, honor, and respect the Holy One of Israel. It doesn't matter if you think that He's Caucasian, Asian, Hispanic, or Black, He remains the Son of the living God, and He is Holy and true. I'm fully aware of my identity – that I'm a Hebrew – but I'm also one who believes that Christ's love extends to all people of all races of all nationalities. So by saying that, I accept this as truth, "To know Him is to love Him and Salvation is free to all that will believe."

When I share my beliefs with people, especially about waiting on God to provide my mate, they think that I am out of my mind. If I have decided to trust God in some areas of my life, why wouldn't I trust Him in all areas since He knows me better than anyone else does?

In my younger days, I was attracted to the thugs, you know the bad boys that could care less about a person's feelings, wants, or needs. As I got older, my desires started changing and then, they changed again, and by the time I was 30, I had a whole new perspective on life.

As you can see, as people we are sometimes here or there and often anywhere, we are constantly evolving.

We want one thing on this day then tomorrow we are on a very different ride.

By saying all of this, I realized that I couldn't trust myself and refused to be heartbroken again by any man. God is truly fragile with my heart, so it was only right to let Him choose one of His sons out of the earth specifically created just for me.

I know that some of you have had a lot of experience in scouting for the right man/woman, but in all of your years of searching, how well has that worked out for you? For those of you who are in happy long-term marriages, I applaud you. But for the rest of us single folk, most beginning relationships are like fairy tales. Your mornings seem to be a little bit brighter, and your day tends to run a lot smoother, all because of this NEW NEW. But how long does that feeling last? A month, a year, or perhaps just a few days, then what eventually happens? You move on to someone more appealing, only to start the cycle all over again. It never ends; you look up and realize that you've wasted a majority of your time on broken, hopeless relationships, and God is saying, "All you had to do was put your trust in Me and be still."

You may feel that waiting on God is a waste of time, but in all actuality, you've already wasted a great deal of your own time. If you wanna see the Glory of God manifest in your life, then give Him His rightful position, not a back burner.

I will be frankly honest with you: It won't be easy. There will be some days when you feel like God has somehow forgotten you. There also may be countless weekends that you will spend alone. Numerous thoughts of that ex will race across your mind. You will try to convince yourself that he wasn't that bad, knowing in the back of your mind that he was NOT it. Never make a permanent decision out of desperate or flared emotions. Desperation does not look good on anyone, it doesn't matter who you are. When I observe some relationships, mostly people I know, I draw the conclusion that makes me think that this person has settled. I never want to get to the end of my life and have major regrets, so settling in my book is never an option (pun intended). Most people settle out of not wanting to be alone, some out of self-unworthiness, and a great deal settle out of convenience.

Imagine marrying someone you don't get along with, just to show off a ring and some wedding pictures. Don't be surprised, there are so many men and women out here who are doing this.

My home girl and I used to play this silly game back then called "Would you marry?" The premise of the game was to ask the question, "Would you marry so-and-so, like a certain celebrity, etc.?" This was just to see if you would marry the most ridiculous person only because they had money, riches, or fame. For example, "Would you marry Bushwick Bill?" If my answer was NO, she'd then up the stakes and add more money to the question by saying, "Ok, would you marry Bushwick Bill if you were given $100,000 up front?" To sum it up, in most cases, my answer would remain NO. It's like this: I cannot see myself stuck for years, let alone life, with someone I don't even like. It would be similar to waking up in prison every day, and on top of that torture, because I'd have to sleep with this person. No, thank you. No amount of money could ever change that.

On nights when I need to hold my pillow and cry, I begin thinking about other people around the world who are in unhealthy marriages or relationships who are crying right now as well, because of so many other different reasons, like physical or verbal abuse, adultery, and abandonment. I thought about the individual who may be dreading their spouse coming home and stirring up a mess due to his/her intoxication. Or the person lying in their bed right now, conjuring up ways to leave. Thoughts like these help me at times due to the fact, it assures me that marriage is not the answer to life and it will never solve all of my problems. Only God can do that. He is the ultimate source.

I'm not the one to whip up a bunch of crap and then throw sugar on it; honestly, I'd prefer the bitter truth over a sweet lie any day. So I won't sit here and say that my journey has been some cool breeze. Many out here will try to sell you a sugarcoated story, and then slap a happy ending on it, but I won't.

To get to this level of keeping it all together took obedience, patience, prayer, hope, and overall steadfast faith.

I did not arrive in this place of tranquility off of some luck and a dream. As humans, we tend to want the easy way out, a shortcut or an exit.

Frankly, there are no shortcuts in life; they just don't exist. You may think that you have found one, but you'll inevitably find yourself at a dead end.

I recently stopped by the store to pick up some cranberry juice, but instead of choosing the one I usually would go for, I decided to try a different brand. The label on the one I chose this time around read "fresh press, (pure) cranberry juice," and it came in a 32-oz. glass bottle as opposed to the usual plastic as the other; its cost was $8.

As I drove home, I decided to open up the juice and take a sip being that the bottle was not that big.

That decision almost caused a major accident! Why? Because this juice was unbearably disgusting, to try to take another sip would be the epitome of agony. The taste was that sick, awfully bitter. I arrived at a stop light harshly stunned by the flavor, which caused me to pick up the bottle again only to read the ingredients. It read, "Enjoy full strength, fresh from whole ripe premium select cranberries." Whew! I was not expecting that! At all!

Well, just think, although it was a better selection, I could not stomach the taste. This juice was in a glass bottle, this juice was natural, this juice didn't have artificial flavor or coloring, this juice even cost more. This juice was authentic and was not watered down in any way. What caused me to go into shock after drinking some of it was the expectation I had from the beginning; due to the other brands I had consumed all of my life. I was used to a little filtered water and a lot of sugar; I was accustomed to it being artificially flavored and from concentrate. Now, let's compare this occurrence with our walk with the Lord. We get used to going to church religiously every Sunday, we get used to praying now and then, we get used to doing a little work for the Lord here and there, but mostly, we get noticeably comfortable with a diluted version of His word. So when we finally get a whiff of what God wants from us, we go into a shock. We can't believe that God wants our whole hearts. We refuse to wrap our minds around being obedient and to top it off, loving our enemies. Our enemies? Oh no. The thought alone leaves us with a bitter taste in our mouths because His wants are so pure.

The Christian life is not a life that calls you to live however you want, it's a way of life that calls you to love, holiness, sanctification, and righteousness. The fantasy of a lot of us women in particular; is to fall in love. The best advice that I can give is to fall in love with Yahushua (Jesus). It troubles me deeply when I hear a woman say "She's (looking) for the right man." Sistahs, let me be the one to tell you that you are out of line. You can look for a lost earring or even your other shoe but; looking for a man? Really?

He who finds a wife finds what is good and receives favor from the Lord.

(Proverbs 18:22)

The only thing a woman who desires her Boaz should be doing is preparing herself and getting herself in position while she waits because when you're ready, according to God's time, he will find you. It's sort of backward for the female to be out hunting for a man rather than have him find her.

Read the story of how Boaz found Ruth. Better yet, read up on the kind of woman Ruth was.

As a woman, making your presence known is quite ok, but anything beyond that may cause a man to lose major respect for you. Stars don't have to struggle to shine. Pressuring a man to marry you or playing these little games can completely turn any good man off. I understand the long-suffering in waiting, most likely better than anyone I know. In my case, it was like someone sitting this big, beautifully wrapped present in front of me and saying, "It's all yours." The problem is, yes, it is mine, but for now, I can't open it; matter of fact; I can't even touch it until the proper time! So what happens in the process? The mind starts to wonder what it could be. In anticipation, I began watching the clock, I started doing all these superficial things to kill time. Sooner or later, I get to a place where I see the gift, I know it's mine, and I become content with the waiting. This is where I am concerning my Boaz and trust it's the best place to be or else I would drive myself insane.

Another thing I have learned about God is, that if He has ordained a certain individual to be with you, then that settles it, he's yours; all you need to do is wait. You will be your husband's crown. Waiting does not involve going out and making a mess of yourself and laboriously attempting to make happen what only

God can piece together. People expect the Lord to bless their mess, not clean up their mess. The Lord is Holy, so if you are to create a mess, or already have a mess and surrender to God, look forward to Him cleaning it up first. God does not dwell in filthy hearts.

This is why so many will not turn to Him, for this simple reason, they have become comfortable with their jacked-up lives. They don't desire change, they only want blessings. It's almost like saying, "OK Lord, give me your best but don't touch my stuff."

I tried Internet mingling a while back, and while creating my page I wrote a message that read, "If you've been digging in the garbage so long till all you know is trash...wrong page." I wrote that because I know we as people get accustomed to junk after we've been stuck in funk for too long. Complacency leaves no room for growth, so you become comfortable in the situation even if it stinks. You are immune to the odor; everyone can smell it, but you. Well, I'm here to let you know that there is a way of escape, out of depression, out of despair, out of this deeply embedded hopelessness that seems to have plagued your brain with thoughts of giving up, even suicide. You've probably tried so many things in this world to numb the pain, only to find that nothing seems to last long enough. You can get drunk and so drugged up but that still will not cut it, because once you sober up, the problem you were running from, still awaits you. NOW TRY JESUS! Pour your soul out to someone who cares. You do not have to face it alone, you can get through this, I sure did and I am happier now than I have ever been in my entire life. Since I have looked loneliness in the face; I no longer Look Lonely in the Face.

We overcome aloneness when we get to a point where we realize that God is all we will ever need.

For where your treasure is, there your heart will be also. (Matthew 6:21)

The light of the body is the eye: if therefore thine eye be single, thy whole body shall be full of light.

But if thine eye is evil, thy whole body shall be full of darkness. If therefore the light that is in thee be darkness, how great is that darkness! (Matthew 6:22)

In Loving Memory of My Grandmother

Delores M. Hagins

www.ingramcontent.com/pod-product-compliance
Lightning Source LLC
LaVergne TN
LVHW051732080426
835511LV00018B/3014